Until Everything Is Continuous Again

UNTIL EVERYTHING IS CONTINUOUS AGAIN

American Poets on the Recent Work
of W. S. Merwin

Edited by Jonathan Weinert
and Kevin Prufer

WordFarm

SEATTLE, WASHINGTON

WordFarm
2816 East Spring Street
Seattle, WA 98122
www.wordfarm.net

Cover Photograph: Robin Holland (www.robinholland.com)
Cover Design: Andrew Craft
This book is typeset in 11pt Apollo MT (Monotype), desgined by Adrian Frutiger

USA ISBN-13: 978-1-60226-011-5
USA ISBN-10: 1-60226-011-7
Printed in the United States of America

First Edition: 2012

Library of Congress Cataloging-in-Publication Data

Until everything is continuous again : American poets on the recent work of W.S. Merwin / edited by Jonathan Weinert & Kevin Prufer. -- 1st ed.
    p. cm.
Includes bibliographical references.
ISBN 978-1-60226-011-5 (pbk.) -- ISBN 1-60226-011-7 (pbk.)
1. Merwin, W. S. (William Stanley), 1927---Criticism and interpretation. I. Weinert, Jonathan, 1959- II. Prufer, Kevin.
 PS3563.E75Z95 2012
 813'.54--dc23

                                     2011043365

P 12 11 10 9 8 7 6 5 4 3 2 1
Y 17 16 15 14 13 12

Contents

Preface

Until Everything Is Continuous Again: American Poets on the Recent Work of W. S. Merwin takes as its subject the poetry of W. S. Merwin since the publication of his twelfth collection, *The Rain in the Trees*, in 1988. The span of over twenty years since can accurately be considered "recent," as the subtitle suggests, only in light of the astonishing length and prodigality of Merwin's career. In the sixty years since W. H. Auden awarded the Yale Younger Poets Prize to Merwin's debut, *A Mask for Janus* (1952), Merwin has published twenty collections of original poems, more than twenty major translations from more than a dozen languages, and eight books of prose, while winning almost every major award that an American poet can win.

The decision to focus on Merwin's eight most recent collections of poems is not arbitrary, nor is it merely chronological. The critical literature on Merwin—surprisingly sparse for a poet of his accomplishments and stature—identifies *The Rain in the Trees* as a watershed in his work, and the foundation for the very different sort of work that he has produced since. Merwin himself has acknowledged that with *The Rain in the Trees* he had "a sense of coming to the feeling that I've done what I wanted to do in that direction, and that the open ground is already somewhere else."

Merwin began exploring that open ground with his next collection, *Travels* (1993). For readers who had come to know his work through the stark, surrealistic, and bereft poems of *The Lice* (1967) and *The Carrier of Ladders* (1970) or through the increasingly casual, intimate, and occasionally ecstatic poems of the 1970s and 1980s, *Travels* was a startling departure. In ways that were not immediately obvious, it also marked a return to the formal rigor, linguistic richness, and cultural engagement of his earliest work.

Establishing that there *is* a recent work stylistically distinct from the preceding work says nothing about the *value* of that recent work, aesthetically or otherwise. In his elegant and closely argued meta-essay on Merwin's book-length narrative poem *The Folding Cliffs* (1998), H. L. Hix contends that no reading of a poem can be complete without inquiring into what that poem puts at stake. Merwin's work, always serious and explicit of purpose, seems especially to invite and reward such inquiry. No matter how small their canvas, how intimate their tone, or how simple their language, the poems of W. S. Merwin keep the question of what is at stake continually in the foreground; they are consistently informed (or haunted) by large, public, and philosophically complex concerns. In response, the essays gathered here concern themselves as much with the social, philosophical, political, and ecological dimensions of Merwin's recent work as with the aesthetic, with the poems as a series of artifacts well or ill wrought.

We'd like to thank several people who contributed to this book's creation. First among them is Jeanie Thompson, who has been, in so many ways, central to the project. Without her ideas, goodwill, and enthusiasm from the very beginning, the book wouldn't exist today. Also we'd like to thank Ruth Goring, who copyedited the book with close attention, speed, and grace, as well as the good people at WordFarm, especially Andrew Craft, Sally Sampson Craft, and Marci Rae Johnson. And finally, each essayist deserves thanks for contributing hours of thought and hard work to this project and, more generally, in the service of American poetry.

Jonathan Weinert
Concord, Massachusetts

Kevin Prufer
Houston, Texas

The Names of the Trees Where I Was Born

From Placelessness to Place in the Poetry of W. S. Merwin

Jonathan Weinert

W. S. Merwin's Migrations

The Moving Target, Finding the Islands, The Compass Flower, Travels, Migration: as these titles of books from every phase of his career attest, W. S. Merwin has always written poems concerned with distances, departures, and journeys. Doubled like the god of its title, the first two poems in Merwin's debut, *A Mask for Janus* (1952),[1] are both named "Anabasis"— a trek into interior country. The term derives from the fifth-century BC account of a Greek mercenary expedition recorded by Xenophon, whose name embeds the Greek root denoting "foreign." As in *The Divine Comedy*, whose *Purgatorio* Merwin would translate almost fifty years into his publishing career, the landscapes that Merwin's poems traverse analogize an inner or metaphysical domain, the passage through which enacts a drama of exile, division, and potential return:

> Still we are strange to orisons and knees.
> Fixed to bone only, foreign as we came,
> We float leeward till mind and body lose
> The uncertain continent of a name.

Merwin's locations may be analogues, but they are not metaphors. They remain, or become, actual locations in the world, even when they are not

specifically named. At the same time, they represent different stages of be-
ing, each with its attendant vision. The darkness or brightness of the vision
depends in part on the perceived distance from a recognized "home"—
"that other land // Estranged almost beyond response."

The sequence of Merwin's collections constitutes a journey that the poet
has undertaken, and each published volume represents a station along his
way—a destination as well as a point of departure. It's no surprise to find
early poems about Odysseus, Columbus, Noah, and the prodigal son, or to
find Merwin addressing a poem to Proteus, since every arrival constitutes
a change of state, or shape. Many critics have written essays that chase
Merwin from book to book, attempting to describe the trajectory of his
"vast mutations," in Richard Howard's phrase.[2] Besides Howard, Charles
Altieri, Cary Nelson, Ed Folsom, Thomas Byers, Marjorie Perloff, Mark
Irwin, and H. L. Hix are among those who have traced continuities and
disjunctions across various phases of Merwin's career.

At times critics have used this approach to decry changes that they
feel deprive the poems of some power that they formerly possessed. Even
Howard, a sympathetic reader of Merwin's early work, seems slightly wist-
ful when detailing the ways in which Merwin's third collection, *Green with
Beasts* (1956),[3] is "so sharply disjunct from [the] initial achievements" of
Merwin's first two books: "[W]e must look hard to see what bearing those
earlier charged counsels of perfection could have on these long looping lines,
these distended paragraphs of slackened expatiation unstarred by any incan-
descence of vocabulary or syntax."[4]

Throughout the 1970s and 1980s, "slackening" was the charge most of-
ten leveled against Merwin by critics uncomfortable with whatever con-
stituted his latest shift in style. To be sure, the arc of Merwin's books from
Writings to an Unfinished Accompaniment (1973)[5] to the watershed volume
The Rain in the Trees (1988)[6] describes a progressive relaxation and light-
ening of diction, form, vision, and even subject matter, unfolding across a
period of more than fifteen years.

A careful examination of his enterprise during this period, however, re-
veals something more than a relinquishing of the tensions that made the
earlier poetry so taut and brilliant: a slow and continuous transforma-
tion from a deep sense of dispossession, division, and placelessness to a

profoundly rooted sense of place and presence, most fully expressed in *The Rain in the Trees*. Over the course of this period, Merwin's poetics completely change their sign, moving from a vision of absence as annihilation to a vision of absence as the paradoxical ground of presence.

To understand how Merwin effected this change, to appreciate the labor and time it cost him to effect it, and to fully comprehend the achievement of *The Rain in the Trees* and its singular position within the long arc of Merwin's work, one must go back to an earlier point, to the first major stylistic shift in Merwin's career.

Journeys Endlessly Deferred

Published in 1963, *The Moving Target*[7] broke from the highly wrought work that preceded it. Merwin's early work—verbally dense, dazzlingly allusive, and rigorously formal—betrays the strong influence of Greek and Latin poetry, the *cançons* of Bernart de Ventadorn, and later mythologizers such as William Blake, Ezra Pound, and Robert Graves. Although the seeds of the change were planted as early as *Green with Beasts*, *The Moving Target* was something entirely new. "[T]he orphic notations, the cryptic aphorisms of René Char stand behind these poems," Richard Howard observes, noting that "the postures of renunciation and impoverishment" in the collection's opening poem "are a suitable prologue to Merwin's new undertaking."[8] This new undertaking saw Merwin progressively undoing "the 'curious-knotted garden' of [his] initial manner" to arrive at the unmistakable (and unpunctuated) style that has been the ground note of his poetry ever since.

Merwin achieves the apotheosis of this new style in *The Lice* (1967)[9] and *The Carrier of Ladders* (1970),[10] the two collections that follow *The Moving Target*. *The Lice*, considered by many to be Merwin's finest and most influential book, is now celebrated as a classic text of the anti–Vietnam War movement, while *The Carrier of Ladders* garnered Merwin the first of two Pulitzer Prizes.

The poem "Plane," which opens *The Carrier of Ladders*, epitomizes Merwin's elegiac "second" style:

Plane

We hurtle forward and seem to rise

I imagine the deities come and go
without departures

and with my mind infinitely divided and hopeless
like a stockyard seen from above
and my will like a withered body muffled
in qualifications until it has no shape
I bleed in my place

where is no
vision of the essential nakedness of the gods
nor of that
nakedness the seamless garment of heaven

nor of any other
nakedness

Here
is the air

and your tears flowing on the wings of the plane
where once again I cannot
reach to stop them

and they fall away behind
going with me

The disconnectedness of airplane travel serves as the literal starting point for an anguished *cri de coeur* that establishes the obsessions that *The Carrier of Ladders* obsessively rehearses. This journey by air is the first of many journeys that are either impossible to make or endlessly deferred—the trains rusted to their tracks in "The Wheels of the Trains," the wagons that never arrive in "The Trail into Kansas," the mountain that doesn't move because it is everywhere in "The Calling under the Breath." In "Plane," any sense of forward movement is immediately attenuated and ultimately subverted. The airplane only "seems" to rise, and in the final couplet the tears that "fall away behind" paradoxically also "hurtle forward" with the plane. This is a journey with no destination, and the speaker's "place" is restricted to a brief and agonized moment of lyric witnessing, suspended precariously in the air above enormous gulfs. If the poem arrives at all, it arrives at an absence, at a place that is no place. "Here / is the air," the poem announces, and the monometer lines slow the poem to a pause.

In the vision of "Plane," a terrible stasis encompasses both heaven and earth: even "the deities come and go / without departures." This stasis is not the stillness of completion or perfection or rest; it is not the "vision of . . . the seamless garment of heaven" but of a "mind infinitely divided and hopeless." The stillness at the heart of the poem does not reveal any "essential nakedness" in which apparent divisions would be swept away in a clear vision of the interconnectedness of all things. Rather, it is the stillness of rigidity, of the defeated will. Except through the impinging consciousness of its absence, the speaker is unable to contact that which he loves and wishes to preserve.

As in much of Merwin's poetry, the loss of self in bewilderment and division shades over into collective loss. The "you" appearing in the poem's penultimate stanza is weeping, as one supposes that the speaker also is weeping, and the lack of specificity here is inclusive, opening out from an implied traveling companion onto the entire world of social relations. All human beings, suspended somewhere between heaven and earth, are hurtling forward in that plane, going nowhere and weeping, and the speaker "cannot / reach to stop" their "tears flowing on the wings of the plane." Drawing the line between personal extinction and the extinctions of animal species and indigenous peoples that appear as persistent concerns in Merwin's work, the poem figures the divided self as "a stockyard seen from above."

"Plane" maps a world of levels and oppositions, such that the title word refers as much to degrees of being as it does to airborne conveyances. The poem suggests presence and absence, a here and an elsewhere, an earth and a heaven, and a silence to which all speech points. In the peculiar sensibility of *The Carrier of Ladders* and much of the poetry leading up to it, absence, elsewhere, heaven, and silence register as more real than presence, here, earth, and speech. "Now all my teachers are dead except silence," Merwin laments in "A Scale in May," in *The Lice*. *The Carrier of Ladders* returns again and again to silence as an abiding presence, as the actual reality behind the apparent reality out of which speech comes and into which it falls.

In her 1970 review of *The Carrier of Ladders*, published in *The New York Times*, Helen Vendler makes much of the "atmosphere" of *The Carrier of Ladders* without inquiring particularly deeply into the metaphysics that produces it:

> [Merwin] is one of the voices singing out of empty cisterns and exhausted wells. . . . [D]esolation and abandonment shading into terror are more common than any other feeling. . . . [O]ne feels that these poems were written not so much from sentiments requiring expression as from obsessive counters demanding manipulation. . . . Is it ill-will in a reader to want to force-feed these pale children till they, when cut, will bleed?[11]

Vendler's view represents a discernible trend in the criticism of what is often referred to as Merwin's middle period. Vendler was not alone in divining parallels between Merwin's "elusive pallors" and T. S. Eliot, specifically "the toneless cry of the Waste Land." To Vendler, Merwin "often seems a lesser Eliot . . . a hollow man finding his hollow divinities."[12] But "Plane" does more than lament a failure of vision that causes a moral failure. Rather, it shows how both of those failures are themselves the effects of existential causes. "Plane" neither blames nor preaches; it *witnesses*, and its refusal to make moral judgments reads as compassion. Here is the insufficiently recognized obverse of the detachment that Vendler and other critics often find so irksome in Merwin's poems, and it suffuses the poems in *The Carrier of Ladders* with a tender, almost supernal light, even when the poems are unremittingly dark.

In the event, Merwin's relentless program of renunciation and impoverishment proved to be an aesthetic and philosophical dead end. In an interview with Ed Folsom and Cary Nelson, conducted in 1981 and 1984, Merwin recounted the extremity of his feelings around the time of writing *The Lice*:

> [M]ost of the time I was writing *The Lice* I thought I had pretty well given up writing, because there was really no point in it. For different reasons— much the same way that I think some writers of continental Europe felt late in the Second World War and after, that there was really no point in

going on writing; what they had experienced was just terrible beyond anything that language could deal with, and there was no point in trying, and there was probably no one to write it for either, for very long.[13]

The danger of literally falling into the silence that these poems both invite and attempt to hold at bay was real. Merwin's poetics were ready for a re-evaluation.

Old Light Going Home

The first evidences of this reevaluation appear almost immediately, in *Writings to an Unfinished Accompaniment*, published just three years after *The Carrier of Ladders*. The poems of this new dispensation, while parallel in diction and form to those that preceded it, sound new notes of relaxation, openness, and invitation. In fact, they register a sea change in Merwin's writing.

The collection opens with a series of short poems startling for their shift in tone. These are not poems of impossible journeys, endless distances, and stasis but poems of possibility—of discovery, relationship, arrival, and change. "All the stones have been us / and will be again," Merwin writes in "Eyes of Summer," inverting Wallace Stevens's assertion that "It is the human that is the alien, / The human that has no cousin in the moon."[14]

"End of Summer" embodies Merwin's emerging vision:

> High above us a chain of white buckets
> full of old light going home
>
> now even the things that we do
> reach us after long journeys
> and we have changed

The vertical and horizontal axes in this poem no longer represent uncrossable distances but rather the dimensions of a vast *now* in which all time is present, bending back on itself in a figure of reconciliation and return. If the "old light going home" is moving away from the speaker's vantage point, the speaker's own history is moving toward him, and it reaches him as the memory of "the things that we do" becomes an agent of change.

Distance has changed its sign; it no longer functions as the spatial correlative of emotional isolation and spiritual division. In "The Distances," distance becomes a reminder "that we are immortal." Distance is sourced in human desire and experience, but nothing is lost in the present informed by memory: "none dies and none is forgotten." Calling begins to evoke response:

> somewhere else the sound
> sound
> will arrive
> light from a star

While still haunted by extinction—"The world is made of less and less / to walk out on farther / and farther"—these poems are full of moments and gestures not available in *The Carrier of Ladders*. Even a poem as fraught as the fourth poem titled "A Door" holds open the possibility that "someone . . . may hear all around us the endless home"; even a poem as dark as "Wanting a Soul in the South" can admit "it's all right though."

In the Folsom and Nelson interview, Merwin describes a shift in attitude that underlies the poems' shift in tone. Folsom asks Merwin to explain "[w]hat happened to the rage and the anger and the despair" that haunted *The Lice* and *The Carrier of Ladders*:

> Oh, I suppose they're still there, but I suppose some lucky recognition that the anger itself could destroy the thing that one was angry in defense of, and that the important thing was to try to keep what Cary described as humility before phenomenal things: the fact that the chair may be destroyed tomorrow is no reason not to pay attention to it this afternoon, you know. The world *is* still around us, and there is that aspect of other human beings which has *not* been solely destructive, and to which one is constantly in debt, and which involves simply the pleasure of existing together, being able to look and see the trees, the cat walking in and out of the room. The answer to even one's anger is in the way one can see those things, the way that one can live with them.[15]

Merwin's "lucky recognition" announces a new focus on perception and the immediacy of presence, and a new impulse to affirm and construct begins to displace the reflex of negation.

If this new impulse did not reach its full expression for another fifteen years, its roots are here. The poem "Exercise" constitutes a sort of manual on perceptual transformation in verse:

> First forget what time it is
> for an hour
> do it regularly every day
>
> then forget what day of the week it is
> do this regularly for a week
> then forget what country you are in
> and practice doing it in company
> . . . .
> forget how to count
> starting with your own age
> starting with how to count backward
> starting with even numbers
> starting with Roman numerals
> starting with fractions of Roman numerals
> starting with the old calendar
> going on to the old alphabet
> going on to the alphabet
> until everything is continuous again
>
> go on to forgetting elements
> starting with water
> proceeding to earth
> rising in fire
>
> forget fire

Paradoxically, Merwin invokes the power of forgetting in the context of a collection that seeks to enact a form of remembering. Paradoxical, too, is a series of commands that calls forth the presence of the things that it instructs the commanded to forget. Like many of Merwin's poems, "Exercise" invokes presence in order to point beyond it—to absence, to the void. Merwin might previously have discerned in this void annihilation or an irrecoverable source. The intent of "Exercise," in contrast, is to suspend the conventions by which we place ourselves in passing time, space, and social reality in order to emerge into an experience of continuity that defeats division and loss.

Something Neoplatonic or kabbalistic can be detected in the closing stanzas, in which the recovery of an originary consciousness beyond the habitual is clearly implied. Phrases such as "fractions of Roman numerals" and the suggestion to forget how to count by starting with the alphabet are designed to short-circuit language and logic. Merwin orchestrates a movement backward from the present moment to Rome and the age of the Desert Fathers, for whom the letters of the alphabet had numerical values that encoded the structure of creation. Could the "old calendar" be the Jewish calendar, which numbers the years since the creation of the world? The poem moves even farther back, to the dawn of language altogether and the ancient conception of a world made of earth, water, fire, and air, then still farther back to the very origins of the universe.

Significantly, the poem asks us to forget earth, water, and fire, but not air. Air is Merwin's element.[16] It is silence and nothingness, but it also gives life and allows speech. "Here / is the air," Merwin is saying again, in another way, but this is not air as void or negation; this is air as total presence, as the unchangeable reality behind the fungible world of appearances.

The Poetics of Place

The three books that follow *Writing to an Unfinished Accompaniment*—*The Compass Flower* (1977),[17] *Finding the Islands* (1982),[18] and *Opening the Hand* (1983)[19]—continue the transformation of outlook heralded by poems such as "Exercise." The titles of the collections alone tell the story of the changes that Merwin's poetry undergoes during these years. *The Compass Flower* superimposes the image of blossoming onto the navigator's compass rose, connoting a flowering that extends in every earthly direction. At the center of the flower stands the observer, the "I," who can both locate himself and find his way. *Finding the Islands* implies that the impossible journey is now in the process of being made, while *Opening the Hand* suggests a sense of release connected with a renewed possibility of interaction and integration, particularly in the realm of human relationships. As Ed Folsom notes, the poems of this period become more colloquial and less gnomic in tone, more clearly narrative and inviting, and more relaxed.[20]

The stylistic changes result from a shift in emphasis. The "poetics of absence" so vividly at work in poems such as "Plane" begins to give way to what Charles Altieri calls a "poetics of place"[21] in which the self, previously wandering in the desert of absence, is able to situate itself and therefore come into existence: "In our traditions . . . selfhood is an affair of presence. One can feel himself integral when, like Robert Creeley, he achieves harmony with the concrete place where he stands and with the desires and objects also occupying or impinging on that place."[22] The place that Merwin finds is half discovered and half invented. It is both the actual island of Maui, Hawai'i, to which Merwin moved in the mid-1970s, and a constructed, imaginative landscape in which desire can find its objects and its ends. Merwin increasingly brings the actual and imaginative landscapes into relationship, superimposing the one upon the other until, in *The Rain in the Trees*, they fuse into a new conception of home.

It is impossible to underestimate the importance of this moment in Merwin's enterprise. For the first time in a poetic career that was already almost three decades long, he turns to the explicit autobiographical details of his life for poetic material. Merwin begins both to embody himself in his poems and to speak more explicitly in his own voice; his poems no longer serve solely as sites of the disembodied voices that had made Helen Vendler so impatient in *The Carrier of Ladders*. To fully inhabit and achieve "harmony with the concrete place," Merwin has to confront the facts of his own life and make them available to his imagination. We find him experimenting with various strategies for reclaiming and refashioning his personal history, including the writing of autobiographical prose, an activity that allows him to address his origins in a more direct manner than he had been able to do before in his poems.

Unframed Originals (1982),[23] Merwin's book of prose recollections from childhood and adolescence, discloses telling parallels between his early life and the abiding atmosphere of his poems. As he describes it, "one of the main themes of *Unframed Originals* is what I was not able to know, what I couldn't ever find out, the people I couldn't meet. . . . [R]eticence was one of the main things I was writing about. Indeed, it was a very reticent family." [24] The sense of a banished totality, of a world as numinous as it was obscure and unreachable, also has roots in Merwin's early experience:

"Once I imagined, with no way of saying it, that my parents, and everyone of their age, kept somewhere among them the whole of the past. They possessed it, and could converse with it at first hand. There were people who existed in another room, which I could not be shown because I was too young. My elders did not talk to me about all this, but they referred to it among themselves."[25] Here it becomes possible to divine the autobiographical sources of Merwin's persistent sense of absence, silence, and exile. If his sensibility was formed by such influences, he would have to define his identity as a poet—a presence effectively made of words—in opposition to them.

The poems of *Opening the Hand*, published less than a year later, derive material directly from *Unframed Originals*. Merwin had written autobiographical poems before, some of which he suppressed and some of which he published—in the concluding section of *The Drunk in the Furnace* (1960),[26] for example—but his relationship to this material was equivocal and irresolute. The thirteen "family" poems that open *Opening the Hand*, in contrast, are remarkably explicit. They are both elegies for and a sort of leave-taking of Merwin's father, a severe and forbidding figure in his recollections. As he confronts his father's memory and bids it farewell, he also bids farewell to his habitual sense of absence, dislocation, silence, and grief.

Edward Brunner writes perceptively about these poems and the change that they mark in Merwin's career. Brunner's reading of "The Houses" articulates the new stance that Merwin assumes toward both his father and the attitudes that his father represents. In this poem, the child, and then the child grown, comes upon an unknown house, but when he tries to show it to his father, the house is not there:

> The father and the son cannot share their feelings; what exists for one is not only invisible to the other but, more harrowingly, what exists when the son is by himself actually vanishes when he tries to share it with his father. . . . That Merwin acknowledges this profound disparity is a sign for change in these family poems, for at the base of his previous work is a compulsive desire to reach out to a father he is trying to understand even as that understanding arrives too late. . . . To move beyond this absorption, one needs to recover a wider perspective which underscores their fundamental separateness.[27]

Merwin recovers this wider perspective by turning away from his father and his father's world. In so doing, he begins to acknowledge his difference from his family not in terms of pain, separation, and the loss of selfhood but in terms of accepting the impossibility of a shared vision.

In the arresting second stanza of "The Oars," the father assumes the position of the "I" of many of the poems in *The Carrier of Ladders*:

> after the century turned   he sat in a rowboat
> with its end on the bank   below the house
> holding onto the oars   while the trains roared past
> until it was time for him   to get up and go

Here the father, rather than the speaker, suffers the stasis of the journey endlessly deferred. The implication is that the speaker has found a way to move on. He can move on in part because he has discovered a place to move *to*. That place is fully established in *The Rain in the Trees*.

A Book Full of Words to Remember

The Rain in the Trees consolidates the new approaches with which Merwin had been experimenting for almost twenty years and grounds them in a newly rooted sense of self, place, and history. The collection includes metaphysical and mythical poems pointing to silence as plenitude, as in *Writings to an Unfinished Accompaniment*; it includes relaxed, colloquial, and immediate poems that would be at home in *The Compass Flower*; it includes tender and at times sentimental love poems, as well as poems of perceptual immediacy, as in *Finding the Islands*; and it includes a fresh set of family poems that extend the autobiographical work of *Opening the Hand*. Interestingly, some of the anger and grief of *The Lice* reappear in the sequence of "Hawaiian" poems toward the end of the collection, as if Merwin's new stance lets him revisit ongoing concerns without becoming trapped in the emotional and aesthetic dead ends that had troubled him before.

By turns incantatory and reportorial, hortatory and resigned, ecstatic and enraged, the poems of *The Rain in the Trees* proceed by means of tensions between the keenly observed and the mystically apprehended, between the almost unbearable elation of finding oneself "wet to the skin and wide awake" and the painful recognition of the destruction of nature and culture that such intense consciousness entails.

Unsurprisingly, images of trees crowd *The Rain in the Trees*. Trees appear as the actual koa, sandalwood, palm, and 'ōhi'a trees of Merwin's adopted Hawai'i. They also appear in figurative guise, as in the world-tree of "The Crust" which "remembered everything" and "whose roots held [the earth] together," and the visionary tree of "Place" which unites the imaginary and the actual and transcends the principle of death.

In a pair of poems with cognate titles, Merwin uses the image of the tree to further articulate the "fundamental separateness" of his sensibility from that of his parents and the world they represent. In "Native Trees" the speaker remembers asking his parents when he was a child "the names of the trees / where I was born," but they can neither hear him nor see the trees to which he points; their attention is held by "surfaces of furniture" and "walls they had forgotten"—dead, superficial, constructed things. The child persists, attempting to establish a connection between his own lineage and the living, rooted world: "Were there trees / where they were children / where I had not been / I asked." But his parents are cut off both from the speaker's perceptions and from their own: "when they said yes it meant / they did not remember." The poem ends with the child's urgent questioning—"What were they I asked what were they"—and the parents' admission of their own ignorance: "but both my mother and my father / said they never knew." Merwin avoids becoming accusatory and achieves a sort of muted compassion, because he implicates his own ignorance as the child of his parents: apparently the child never knew the names of the trees either, and there's nothing in this poem to suggest that he ever bothered to find out.

When Merwin does name the trees later on, in "Native," the trees he names are not those of his own childhood or his parents'; crucially, they are the trees of his adopted home. The trees in "Native" are, in fact, the rare and endangered species that Merwin has planted on his property in Ha'ikū, on Maui: "here seeds from destroyed valleys / open late / beside their names in Latin / in the shade of leaves I have put there." The names of these trees substitute for "the names of the trees / where I was born," as the adopted place becomes the site of the self's imaginatively constructed home. The speaker in the poem becomes a sort of Adam, tending a garden and assigning names to the lives that dwell there. But if this is an Eden, it is a late Eden, growing seeds from valleys already destroyed, bearing within it the consciousness of loss and time.

The project of *The Rain in the Trees* rests on contradictions such as this. There is a sense that things can be seen and cared for only against the background of their disappearance, that love can be found only in the awareness of its vanishing, that a community can be established only from the remnants of a decimated culture, and that language can serve as a means of connection only in the recognition of how insufficient and diminished it has become as a tool of material and cultural misappropriation. Even Merwin's sense of himself as a conscientious witness is contradictory: as much as he may rail against them, he implicates himself in the litany of man-made things—rooms, airports, cars, skyscrapers, real estate speculation, politics—responsible for the ongoing destruction of the earth, acknowledging that he is also a citizen of "the known world / which it is hopeless to reject / and death to accept."

The extraordinary poem "History" serves as a kind of doorway or gate out of *The Rain in the Trees* into the new sorts of poems that Merwin would start writing in *Travels* (1993)[28] and the books that followed. The speaker no longer confronts a journey that he cannot make; rather, he is on a journey from which he cannot return. As has Merwin in his life, the speaker in "History" adopts the stance of the eternal visitor who carries not only his own memories but also the memories of the communities in which he dwells as both witness and foreigner. Merwin achieves a synthesis of detachment and immediacy, loss and survival, that informs the increasingly personal, complex, and historically oriented narratives he would write throughout the 1990s, culminating in *The Folding Cliffs* (1998),[29] a book-length poem concerning the nineteenth-century history of Kaua'i, and his verse translation of Dante's *Purgatorio* (2000).[30]

The speaker's position in "History" is, in fact, precisely that of Dante in Purgatory: he is of the earth, or once was, but now finds himself visiting the earth as a stranger. It is only from this uncanny distance that the speaker, like Dante, can truly begin to *see*:

Only I never came back

the gates stand open
where I left the barnyard in the evening
as the owl was bringing the mouse home
in the gold sky
at the milking hour
and I turned to the amber hill and followed
along the gray fallen wall
by the small mossed oaks and the bushes of rusting
arches bearing the ripe
blackberries into the long shadow
and climbed the ancient road
through the last songs of the blackbirds

These lines, among Merwin's most sublime, feature many characteristics typical of the more recent poems: a depopulated historical landscape, often agrarian, in the process of reverting to wilderness; a wanderer, solitary or in agreeable company, haunted by the ghosts of the peoples who have vanished from the landscape and whose soliloquy we overhear; a voice rooted in the cadences of ordinary speech but aspiring to the condition of song; keen observation and compressed description; simple language and exceptional clarity of surface.

As is often the case in Merwin's recent work, the simplicity of the passage is merely apparent; there is submerged structure, paradox, and literary allusion that the beauty of the lines tends to mask. Like the Eden imagined in "Native," the Edenic scene of "History" is shot through with the sense of its inevitable passing even as the speaker constructs the lines with which he intends to secure its representation. The poem's occasion is the speaker's (presumably final) departure from the place it describes; "the amber hill" is countered by "the gray fallen wall," "the ripe / blackberries" are swallowed by "the long shadow" into which they grow, and the "gold sky / at the milking hour" is counterbalanced by "the last songs of the blackbirds." These figurations refer directly to Wallace Stevens in his valedictory mode, as well as to the odes of Keats. The sequence of colors, from gold to amber to gray to black, recapitulates the "downward to darkness" movement at the end of "Sunday Morning," with blackbirds, that most Stevensian of species, standing in for pigeons. The rusted autumnal landscape, the mossed trees and ripe fruit, the barnyard animals, the encroaching shadows and gathering birds transpose the scene of Keats's "To Autumn." The poem proceeds from sky to hill to wall to road, from the present through long shadows to an ancient right-of-way, underscoring the direction in which Merwin's compass consistently points: toward the demotic and the deeply rooted, toward the earth and the past.

By opening the poem with a line that syntactically should appear at the end of the poem—in the order of sense, the poem's first line, "Only I never came back," should follow the poem's last line, "I was not going to be long"—Merwin employs a structural pun that seeks to defeat the passage of time. The speaker's claim that he never returned is made to serve as the means by which a return to the lost place is initiated in memory and representation. The fragment's syntax, separated so far from its context, becomes eloquently ambiguous: Does "only I" mean simply "but I," or does it mean "I and I alone," implying that others, or perhaps the very scenes that the speaker describes, *did* in fact come back?

The final three stanzas of "History" address the ambivalence toward language that Merwin has expressed throughout his career:

> there was a note on a page
> made at the time
> and the book was closed
> and taken on a journey
> into a country where no one
> knew the language
>
> no one could read
> even the address
> inside the cover
> and there the book was
> of course lost
>
> it was a book full of words to remember
> this is how we manage without them
> this is how they manage
> without us
>
> I was not going to be long

In "The First Year," which appears earlier in the collection, language erects a screen that interposes between the self and its deepest apprehensions. Only by moving into the silence beyond language can the self experience renewal and the clarity of pure perception: "When the words had all been used / for other things / we saw the first day begin." But in "History," Merwin does more than point to a numinous experience beyond language. He extends and, to a certain extent, reverses the skepticism about language that has haunted him at least since *The Lice*. The "book full of words to remember" (that is, words that support the act of remembering) has been lost in a foreign country—lost for good, since no one in that country can speak the language and the book cannot be returned. The note written on a page of that book, the sign of an individual's response to a significant communication, has also been lost. It is a version of the necessary but inaccessible text that the pencils in "The Unwritten" won't "unroll," in *Writings to an Unfinished Accompaniment*.

Here, however, Merwin does not rest with mourning the loss of intelligibility. While the rest of "History" is written in the past tense, the three penultimate lines are in the present tense: "this is how we manage without them / this is how they manage / without us." These lines serve as the speaker's own gloss on the poem's meaning, and they place the act of linguistic representation within the context of an ongoing struggle to live a tolerable life despite the uncertain ability of language to articulate a web of intelligible interconnections. The "this" to which the lines refer is indefinite, suggesting a number of alternative readings. "This" may refer to the way we carry on living despite the tragedies and losses we endure every day. "This" may also refer more specifically to the poem itself, and, by extension, to the entire enterprise of poetic representation, which the poem questions.

Merwin's misgivings about language also have social and cultural dimensions. He wishes to speak for all those peoples who have lost their languages—either because of the passage of time, as in "Pastures," or because of cultural genocide, as in "Losing a Language" and "The Lost Originals." He is sensitive to the irony inherent in an outsider attempting to use the usurper's own tongue to speak on behalf of the dispossessed. But he stakes out common ground by pointing to the experiences of loss and elation that are common to all human beings, and he attempts to fashion an imaginative language that can account for those common experiences. "There is an individual relationship between the human imagination and all of life," Merwin remarked before a reading, predominantly of poems from *The Rain in the Trees*, in May 2011, "and that relation is the basis of human compassion. . . . The only attitude that includes everything, the whole of life, is to realize that we are all here together."[31] Here Merwin approaches the "vision of . . . / the seamless garment of heaven" that was denied in *The Carrier of Ladders* and prefigured in *Writings to an Unfinished Accompaniment*—a vision in which there is no division, and everything is continuous again.

To Merwin

The Ode as Tautology in *Present Company*

Lisa Russ Spaar

Odal fire has been one of W. S. Merwin's modes as far back as *A Mask for Janus* (1952).[1] "Ode: The Medusa Face" introduces into that formally intrepid, dazzling showcase of a first book the fluid, heuristic, metaphysical Zen-prayer version of the classical poem of agon and apostrophe that strikes me as the most expressive, essential manifestation of Merwin's vision. Why, then, did it take me so long—decades of my own ongoing apprenticeship—to warm to Merwin's work? And what was it about encountering *Present Company* (2005), a collection of one hundred and one lyrics beginning with the word "To" ("To the Tongue," "To the Consolations of Philosophy," "To Zbigniew Herbert's Bicycle," "To the Thief at the Airport," "To the Middle," "To Glass," "To the Smell of Water"), that at last awakened me to the subtle plangency of Merwin's sensibility, his inimitable way of wielding and surrendering to language, which I now realize, in retrospect, has haunted my imagination and stalked my reading and writing of poetry for nearly as long as I have been attempting both?[2]

It was impossible to study contemporary poetry as an undergraduate in the early to mid-1970s and not confront W. S. Merwin's work. Everyone I knew who wrote poetry seriously carried around a copy of Merwin's sixth book, *The Lice* (1967), in a well-worn two-tone paperback edition, invariably dog-eared at three Ur-poems that seemed to represent the zeitgeist of the times: "For the Anniversary of My Death," "Some Last Questions," and "The Asians Dying.[3] The Merwin I first knew was not the maker of "engines of order, of artifice, of ornament," as Richard Howard characterized much of the early work, but the poet of what Howard would go on to call the "cool radiance" of his middle period that "[invited] the participation of [the] silence . . . he once warded off with all the words in his armory."[4]

Merwin's influence on poets at that time cannot be understated. His early midcareer vocabulary of loss and mutability—what Howard refers to as his "asymptotic phenomenology of thresholds, doors, passages, 'the gates about to close / that never do,'" and which Helen Vendler iterated as his "dictionary . . . of ill omen (pain, grief, fear, pallor, extinction), obsessive objects (gloves, hands, clocks, watches, bandages, shrouds, eyes), exhausted adjectives (hollow, empty, faint, deaf, blind, blank, frozen, lost, broken, hungry, dead), and constellations of negation (speechless, colorless, nameless, windless, unlighted, unseen, unmoved, unborn)"—was pervasive.[5] By late in the decade, words like "darkness" and "stone" and "light" were already beginning to feel like parodic *mots-valises*. (I remember an underground newspaper at Brown publishing a lampoon titled something like "How to Write a *New Yorker* Poem," which admonished the poet to make a mandatory reference to shadows and water, use the phrase "as if," and indulge in a tone of oracular and sincere detachment.) Is it possible, then, that I resisted on some level (youthful jealousy? insecurity about my own incipient poems? a tendency to mistrust popular opinion?) Merwin's precocious and prolific oeuvre (which included by then books of translations as well as plays), his rapidly rising star, his ubiquitous influence on my teachers and peers?

A more honest explanation for my disquietude would be that I wasn't yet ready for Merwin. Perhaps for the same reason that I was unable in those years to concentrate during yoga class or would rather have been shot with tacks than accompany a group of friends to a spa featuring immersion in the natal seawater of isolation tanks, Merwin's dilated rhetorical gestures, his reliance on abstraction, his improvisation on a closely keyed accessible lexicon, his willingness to repeat himself ("you say nothing / once"), his accrual of subordinate clauses and way of slipping out of his skin and eluding any one point of view, his formal and often seemingly bodiless and extrahuman shape-shifting, created in me a restive anxiety. Ephemeral, umbral, often unpunctuated, borrowing the oneiric motion of clouds, blades, and mirrors, those poems—plainspoken and philosophical—had the feel of ideograms, of water evaporating on a hot sidewalk, of the body's double swallowed or effaced by darkness. Infatuated as I was (and remain) with print, text, orthography, the poem's materiality on the page, and with the brocaded, physical, impassioned textures, the "fine excess" of sensory image and strife, of Dickinson, Keats, Shakespeare's plays, and Hopkins, I was not yet prepared to appreciate the quieter detonations of Merwin's invitation, his *via negativa*, his gift:

> I call to it Nameless One O Invisible
> Untouchable Free
> I am nameless I am divided
> I am invisible I am untouchable
> and empty
> nomad live with me
> be my eyes
> my tongue and my hands
> my sleep and my rising
> out of chaos
> come and be given

In 2005, however, I sought out *Present Company*, mainly because I'd run across poems from its contents before the book was published in places like *Poetry*, *The American Poetry Review*, and *The New Yorker*. I had been particularly impressed by Merwin's poems that appeared in the wake of the Twin Towers tragedy of September 2001—"To the Words," for example, which I read in the October 8, 2001, issue of *The New Yorker* and which struck me with the force of its interior polis. So much political and occasional poetry lapses into proselytizing, but Merwin's "you" conflated the odal speaker, the dead, the Ancient of Days, the poem, you, me, in a way that felt urgent, authentic, vulnerable, and immediate:

When it happens you are not there

O you beyond numbers
beyond recollection
passed on from breath to breath
given again
from day to day from age
to age
charged with knowledge
knowing nothing

"Somewhere between the public ode of the epithalamion and the private ode of self-reflection," writes poet and classicist Carl Phillips, "there's the ode of intimate dialogue, known as prayer . . . [and behind] any prayer, of course, is the ongoing agon between gods and humans, the imbalance of power that makes prayer necessary. But as well, prayer commonly springs from crisis, from a struggling to which there seems no earthly resolution."[6] Suddenly, perhaps because of the unsettling tensions of the autumn 2001 crisis that occasioned those poems, my own aging, and my growth as a reader and as a poet, I saw that Merwin's long resistance, syntactically, rhetorically, aesthetically, to expectations and answers, and his creation of an in-the-moment, visionary rhetorical praxis, was his way, as Howard puts it, of "becoming a vehicle for vision, rather than a manipulator of it."[7]

I was intrigued as well by the way the sprinkling of Merwin's "To" poems that I came across in magazines and journals in the first part of the new millennium both apostrophized and lauded their subjects, but also, by playing on that preposition, suffused the poems with a sense of quiet compulsion or admonition ("into the breach!"—or Rilke's "onward, onward, no lakes until eternity"—the *to* that propels us the way the sun goes, as Charles Wright puts it). The mix of still, Keatsian, meditative *lyric attention* and a concurrent *narrative urgency* of poems like "To the Words" struck me as possessing clues to the Merwin mystery that had eluded me for years. Finally, the book's title, *Present Company*, when it appeared, seemed haunted by the phantom "excepted" of the cliché phrase "present company excepted." Would I feel excluded from Merwin's present companions in this book, or included, invited, inspired?

Present Company showed me how to read Merwin. For one thing, these poems of apostrophe, attention, petition, and praise suggested and suggest to me that whether overtly noted or not, most of Merwin's poems are odes. (And as Carl Phillips puts it, what poem is *not* an ode?) The ode, writes Stanley Plumly,

> invites memory and crosses borders; it acquires a past—historical or mythical—while focusing its attention on the drama of the present tense. . . . All poems, at heart, *feel*; the ode, though, seems to want to think and think through its event as well. Odes, in their embodiment, want to involve as much of the whole body and brain as possible. They, in fact, build a collateral body, in a form that emulates the process of that building. . . . They teach us that the modern lyric has no announced beginning or ending, only the long contemplative moment in between.[8]

Yes! Feeling *and* thinking, and more thinking than usual, capturing the numinous and fleeting motion of a mind in the act of being: doubting, intuiting, rethinking through all of the infinitesimal fluxes of consciousness. In a way I hadn't had access to before, I began to see the prescient voltas in Merwin's work, which had sometimes seemed ungrounded, as deep hinges of emotion and perception. The touchstone poem "To Age," for example, with its crush of awarenesses, its ecstatic shifts in perspective and scale, creates a mimetic effect of the unfathomable and yet acutely somatic experience of time dilating nonlinearly into all of our ages:

> It is time to tell you
> what you may have guessed
> along the way without
> letting it deter you
> do you remember how
> once you liked to kneel looking
> out of the back window
> while your father was driving
> and the thread then of pleasure
> as you watched the world appear
> on both sides and from under
> you coming together
> into place out of nowhere
> growing steadily longer

and you would hum to it
not from contentment but
to keep time with no time
floating out along it
seeing the world grow
smaller as it went from you
farther becoming longer
and longer but still there
well it was not like that
but once it was out of sight
it was not anywhere
with the dreams of that night
whether remembered or not
and wherever it was
arriving from on its way
through you must have been growing
shorter even as you
watched it appear and go
you still cannot say how
but you cannot even tell
whether the subway coming
in time out of the tunnel
is emerging from
the past or the future

It is possible, in fact, that each poem in *Present Company*—whether strophic, epistolary, sonnet-haunted, riddlelike, epigrammatic, or longer and more sprawling—might be read provocatively with either the title "To Life" or "To Death," Merwin's twin polestars, his flood subjects. All of Merwin's big themes are here, and the book could serve as a breviary and Baedeker for his mercurial and protean career. Is it too much to posit that the odes in *Present Company* offer us Keats's seven-month odal project writ large? In any case, whether the subject at hand is one's lost teeth, a mosquito, or the poet's wife, the dedicatory "to" in Merwin's odes is stalked always by the migrant, primal movement we must, all of us, make away to our own ends: acceptance, poetry, our mortality.

Fittingly, *Present Company* takes as its arc the motions of nature—a diurnal/nocturnal passage from dawn to dusk to dawn, and the cycle of the seasons, beginning in spring and moving through summer, fall, and winter, culminating at the cusp of the new year. The ontological opening poem, "To This May," which evokes, acoustically, "To Dismay," but also the familiar epistolary address "To [whom] this may [concern]" (Merwin's letter to the world), marvels that

> here
> it is spring once more with its birds
> nesting in the holes in the walls
> its morning finding the first time
> its light pretending not to move
> always beginning as it goes

In "To the New Year," near the book's conclusion, Merwin writes

> so this is the sound of you
> here and now whether or not
> anyone hears it this is
> where we have come with our age
> our knowledge such as it is
> and our hopes such as they are
> invisible before us
> untouched and still possible

Merwin extends this train of thought in the book's very last poem, "To the Book," a meta-address to the object itself, to the words between their covers sifting like sand, like water, through our hands, belonging as much to everything *not us* as they ever belonged to the author or the "you" he's been addressing (one thinks here of Merwin's beloved Thomas Wyatt: "I leve of therefore, / Sins in a nett I seke to hold the wynde")[9]:

> Go on then
> in your own time
> this is as far
> as I will take you
> I am leaving your words with you
> as though they had been yours
> all the time

of course you are not finished
how can you be finished
when the morning begins again
or the moon rises
even the words are not finished
though they may claim to be

never mind
I will not be
listening when they say
how you should be
different in some way
you will be able to tell them
that the fault was all mine

whoever I was
when I made you up

Stanley Plumly writes, "Whatever the occasion or emotion generating the modern lyric—love or loss or both—the mind of the poem owes its heart to the ode, the pensive part of us, the imagination standing before a small fire, looking into it."[10] The odes in *Present Company*, each an intense flame, opened me afresh to Merwin's *openness*—to the fluid exchange and friction of order and oblivion at work in his language: to the white heat of his vision. Importantly, this book revealed to me something I had not been able to see before: Merwin's agon, his struggle—what Carl Phillips calls "the constantly-in-flux human psyche and the human impulse to contain flux. The poem as the occasion of temporary restraint, a restraint we at once want and don't want. The ode as but a form of that strange occasion."[11] One effect of these apostrophic, unpunctuated odes—quotidian, elegiac, laudatory, admonitory, loving—is that they make of questions a kind of answer:

Is anyone there
if so
are you real
either way are you
one or several

> if the latter
> are you all at once
> or do you take turns not answering

Revisiting Merwin's work in my own midlife, I realize that his poetry—its cadences, its negative capabilities—has been with me ever since I began to make poems, and for that, and for the open invitation to be present to his work anew, I am grateful.

> You have brought me once more to the old house
> After all these years of remembering
>   Without knowing
>
> It was you who kept opening the way

Origin, Presence, and Time in the Work of W. S. Merwin

Mark Irwin

The keen sense of origin in W. S. Merwin's poetry, especially in the later work after his move to Hawai'i, is and has always been linked to absence, that "paradise" where things continually vanish from human time. It is the notion of presence, however, closely linked with absence, that provides the *all-at-onceness* of the senses in Merwin's work and thus creates paradox. The poet comments on this in an interview, included in this volume: "The more present you try to make the moment, the more absent it becomes, although it becomes something you can deal with. The present is something that you can't get closer to, and yet that's what you're trying to do with speech—you're trying to embody the present and pass it on at the same time."

One hears this echo in the collection *Present Company* (2005), especially in "To Absence," the poet's invocation to loss and the resurrection of the present through memory.[1] The poem begins with the line "Raw shore of paradise" and asks:

> what good to you
> are the treasures beyond
> words or number
> that you seize forever
> unmapped imperium

when only here
in the present
which has lost them
only now
in the moment you
have not yet taken
does anyone know them
or how rare they are

The "unmapped imperium" or empire of loss that Merwin invokes is starkly juxtaposed to the present, that fleeting time in which we perceive and begin to know things. Reminding us that we often only experience the world through loss, the poem resounds with paradox and suggests that a great deal of human consciousness occurs in memory. In "Learning a Dead Language," a poem from *Green with Beasts* (1956), the speaker says, "What you remember saves you. To remember / Is not to rehearse, but to hear what never / Has fallen silent."[2] This earlier poem also accentuates the paradox of all language, and especially of poetry: an attempt to capture the present through the antiquity of words and grammar.

                    To understand
The least thing fully you would have to perceive
The whole grammar in all its accidence
And all its system, in the perfect singleness
Of intention it has because it is dead.

The palm forest in Hawai'i that the poet restored from a ruined pineapple plantation in the 1980s, and still cultivates, provides a strong insight into the poet's themes of origin and absence, for all gardens are a metaphor of that which is continually dying and coming back to life. "On the Subject of Poetry," a resonant poem from *The Dancing Bears* (1954), locates one source in Merwin's work and further illumines his more recent poetry.[3] Here, just as later, this poet's uncanny ability to *listen* summons the present, and by doing so overrides the haunting world of indeterminacy that arises from expectation or memory. Here is the poem in its entirety:

On the Subject of Poetry

I do not understand the world, Father.
By the millpond at the end of the garden
There is a man who slouches listening
To the wheel revolving in the stream, only
There is no wheel there to revolve.

He sits in the end of March, but he sits also
In the end of the garden; his hands are in
His pockets. It is not expectation
On which he is intent, nor yesterday
To which he listens. It is a wheel turning.

When I speak, Father, it is the world
That I must mention. He does not move
His feet nor so much as raise his head
For fear he should disturb the sound he hears
Like a pain without a cry, where he listens.

I do not think I am fond, Father,
Of the way in which always before he listens
He prepares himself by listening. It is
Unequal, Father, like the reason
For which the wheel turns, though there is no wheel.

I speak of him, Father, because he is
There with his hands in his pockets, in the end
Of the garden listening to the turning
Wheel that is not there, but it is the world,
Father, that I do not understand.

Once again origin is linked to absence. Poetry, which is born from percep-
tion, eschews knowledge because facts tend toward completion. Perception
on the other hand, no matter how keen, finds only the partial, ghostly,
and present. In a 2010 essay, "The House and Garden: The Emergence of a
Dream," Merwin writes, "No story, though, begins at the beginning. The
beginning does not belong to knowledge."[4] The beginning, so present-
ripe, often takes us unaware and lies beyond perception and the power
of language.

The mythic power of "On the Subject of Poetry" arises as the poet listens "To the wheel revolving in the stream, only / There is no wheel there to revolve." The wheel becomes an axis of the unheard and silence from which all poetry arises, and as in all of Merwin's most profound poems, the paradox that arises is born from the words themselves: the poet's attempt to capture the present through the age of language. Merwin comments on this in an interview from 1999:

> The moment you say *paradox,* you're using language to express something that cannot be expressed, and that's what poetry is: There is nothing but presence; on the other hand, there seems to be nothing but absence, and poetry is addressing this emerging presence, this speaking presence, but actually everything that we think of in the phenomenal world is absence. It's the past and future. Very few things are actually present.[5]

Similarly in "On the Subject of Poetry," the man strives to invoke this difficult presence while attempting to reject both the future and past: "It is not expectation / On which he is intent, nor yesterday / To which he listens. It is a wheel turning." This art of listening is sometimes painful and difficult to master—something we sense as the poet gradually becomes the speaker:

> I do not think I am fond, Father,
> Of the way in which always before he listens
> He prepares himself by listening.

Merwin artfully gathers the ineffable through the repetition of five words (*father / garden / wheel / listen / world*) in five stanzas of five lines. The poem ends as absence and distance approach each other. Here the speaker becomes the poem's protagonist in quest of the unutterable, the phenomenal world "in the end of the garden," and the speaker is unable to understand since the world is most often conveyed in words. The paradox of one sitting "in the end of March" and "in the end of the garden" suggests that prenascent time before germination, filled with an absence foreboding presence.

Through the creation of an illusory wheel and an intangible garden, Merwin reminds us of what Aristotle demanded from poetry of the highest order: "the poet's function is to describe, not the thing that has happened, but a kind of thing that might happen, i.e., what is possible as being probable or necessary."[6] Furthermore, the poet's treatment of words like "Father," "wheel," and "garden" raise language to a higher power and echo Emmanuel Levinas's notion of *illeity*, one of the highest expectations of language. He suggests that the true function of a word is not its finite ability to convey information but its reach for infinity: "for it bears witness to the glory of the infinite."[7]

Merwin has said, "Poetry always begins and ends with listening," and again listening becomes the topic of "The Nomad Flute," a poem from *The Shadow of Sirius* (2008), written over fifty years later than "On the Subject of Poetry."[8] Perhaps inspired by *Eighteen Songs of a Nomad Flute*, a suite of poems about the Han Dynasty poet Cai Wenji, who was captured as a young wife by Xiongnu nomads, Merwin's poem haunts absence in both a historic and a present sense. The poem seems not only a subtle lament for the losses of Cai Wenji, but also an invocation to the Muse as the poet ages:

> You that sang to me once sing to me now
> let me hear your long lifted note
> survive with me

"The Nomad Flute" initiates the collection *The Shadow of Sirius*, and here the Dog Star, the brightest in the night sky, assumes a mythic status grounded deeply in the personal, since several of the poems in this collection are elegies for the author's beloved chows. Additionally, this shadow of the brightest star echoes a number of paradoxes in Merwin's work. Personal loss is the "Raw shore of paradise," something we strive to resurrect in memory, yet loss also takes the form of things we do not know or haven't done; we just aren't aware of them. "The Nomad Flute" ends with a final couplet that defies age through the timeless and regenerative quality of poetry, joining the new with the ancient:

> I have with me
> all that I do not know
> I have lost none of it
>
> but I know better now
> than to ask you
> where you learned that music

where any of it came from
once there were lions in China

I will listen until the flute stops
and the light is old again

Merwin's work, whose subject over the course of sixty years seems to move from place to displacement and then to *all-encompassing* place, might finally be seen as the *Georgics* of a kind of contemporary Virgil, although one whose hero might be viewed as the diasporic voice looking for a place in the natural world not maimed by industry, greed, and the commodification of desire, perhaps the most devastating crisis of this past and present century. Many readers will rightly find Merwin's mythic voice as some originary guardian of earth and animal spirits, and by "originary" I also mean the uncanny power of genesis or swift *coming-into-existence* that his poems engender.

Place

On the last day of the world
I would want to plant a tree

what for
not for the fruit

the tree that bears the fruit
is not the one that was planted

I want the tree that stands
in the earth for the first time

with the sun already
going down

and the water
touching its roots

in the earth full of the dead
and the clouds passing

one by one
over its leaves

In his memorable and sacred "Place," from *The Rain in the Trees* (1988), Merwin re-creates a sense of origin and timelessness, one brutally destroyed by capitalism in recent decades.[9] The poem's first two lines, each with seven monosyllabic words, seem to compose a miniature poem, a sonnet of fourteen words, complete with volta, or turn of thought, after the first line:

On the last day of the world
I would want to plant a tree

Deftly collapsing temporal and spatial boundaries, the poem creates a memory in the future, a kind of jarring paradox that recalls Merwin's "The Last One," a poem from *The Lice* (1967) in which the shadow of the last tree becomes a dark monument for our future.[10] Here, however, the speaker conjures hope through a voice washed of ego, a voice whose powers of transformation are linked to stance, vision, and a conscience that protects the natural world and its creatures, a voice with biblical echoes but whose praxis comes from firsthand experience (regularly planting trees in the conservancy), a voice that speaks from the earth and beyond, recalling lines from the Bhagavad Gita that remind us that gratification lies in action, not reward:

not for the fruit

the tree that bears the fruit
is not the one that was planted

In his "The Origin of the Work of Art," Heidegger argues that in enduring art there is often a continual exchange and communion between earth and sky. Merwin's poem ends as the tree joins earth (*roots / dead*) with the sky (*leaves / clouds*), engendering a moment of eternity. Thus the tree becomes an *axis mundi*, a cosmic axis that links creation with destruction, beginning with end, and transcends that end through the act of giving. Merwin has created myth of the highest order: a tree that teaches us how to live in the world.

David Brower, the renowned environmentalist, talks about wilderness as the original place within the imagination, and throughout Merwin's later work there's a pervasive sense of the wild that manifests itself both in content and through stylistic devices such as the poet's unpunctuated lines. "In wildness is the preservation of the world," Thoreau says,[11] and it is Merwin's deep respect for origins in the vegetal and animal world that finally leads to his ability to expand place from root to star and to capture the dissolving sense of the present, also filled with absence, in which all time abides in its expansiveness. One first glimpses this expansiveness in an earlier poem, "Finding a Teacher," from *Writings to an Unfinished Accompaniment* (1973).[12] The poem begins "In the woods I came on an old friend fishing / and I asked him a question." Later, however, we realize this is no regular question but one of metaphysical urgency that leaps from the personal toward the cosmic:

> it was a question about the sun
>
> about my two eyes
> my ears my mouth
> my heart the earth with its four seasons
> my feet where I was standing
> where I was going

The poem ends with a signature note of absence hinting at a Zen koan:

> I no longer knew what to ask
> I could tell that his line had no hook
> I understood that I was to stay and eat with him

Merwin's poems are nothing less than transformative as they question the ineffable with uncanny gestures of negative capability. "Du mußt dein Leben ändern," they sometimes suggest in whispers. "You must change your life," in the words of Rilke, who believed that "singing is being."

A further orchestration of origin, presence, and time can be seen in Merwin's capacious "Just This" from *The Shadow of Sirius.* Here pre-existence merges with existence and the multiplicity of place, from origin of the universe to bodily cell to constellation. They gather all time, while somewhat miraculously this ongoing creation is "read by lightning" as we read it on the page:

Just This

When I think of the patience I have had
back in the dark before I remember
or knew it was night until the light came
all at once at the speed it was born to
with all the time in the world to fly through
not concerned about ever arriving
and then the gathering of the first stars
unhurried in their flowering spaces
and far into the story the planets
cooling slowly and the ages of rain
then the seas starting to bear memory
the gaze of the first cell at its waking
how did this haste begin this little time
at any time this reading by lightning
scarcely a word this nothing this heaven

In 1999 Merwin commented on this notion of the present, a notion that seems clearly linked to his ability to dilate the present until it contains all time:

> The present is the primary thing. The absolute primary thing, but every-thing else is secondary and relative as you try to deal with it. Our relation to it is dissolving. The present in a sense doesn't exist in time. I really believe that the beginning of the universe is still there. The universe in a sense has not begun, and that beginning is there in every moment of the present.[13]

The notion that "the beginning of the universe is there in every moment of the present" is fascinating and provides a key insight into the poet's imagi-nation. In a sense "the present" makes everything possible through the art of attention, and Merwin's art here presences itself with the perception of the entire universe in its evolution.

Moving from darkness and pre-memory toward light, the poet captures the ephemeral notion of time as it is unfolding: "the light came / all at once

at the speed it was born to / with all the time in the world to fly through."
He is able to capture these ephemerae in part through the complex yet
unadorned decasyllabic lines that are both unpunctuated and enjambed.
Moreover, the use of words ending in "ing," functioning as participles,
gerunds, and adjectives, suspends and further dilates the moment:

> not concerned about ever arriving
> and then the gathering of the first stars
> unhurried in their flowering spaces

Finally, it's important to mention something about Merwin's work that I
believe distinguishes it from most other poetry. There is an aura about this
poem and many others akin to the light in Vermeer or Rembrandt paint-
ings, and there is an original music that comes from very high and far away,
something this poet once hinted at forty years ago, when he said poetry
might be likened "to an unduplicatable resonance, something that would
be like an echo except that it is repeating no sound."[14]

A Forgotten Language

Eric Pankey

Absence (and the finding of a language to embody it) is and has been a recurring concern in W. S. Merwin's poetry. I want to consider his 1988 collection *The Rain in the Trees*, but to do so I want to recall my first encounter with Merwin's amazing 1967 collection, *The Lice,* and, in particular, the poem "When You Go Away":

> When you go away the wind clicks around to the north
> The painters work all day but at sundown the paint falls
> Showing the black walls
> The clock goes back to striking the same hour
> That has no place in the years
>
> And at night wrapped in the bed of ashes
> In one breath I wake
> It is the time when the beards of the dead get their growth
> I remember that I am falling
> That I am the reason
> And that my words are the garment of what I shall never be
> Like the tucked sleeve of a one-armed boy[1]

In retrospect, one can recall moments of learning, of insight, when in an instant what had been opaque suddenly radiates its clarity and candor. Up until the moment of encountering this poem, I had assumed that originality was, for lack of a better word, novelty. In Ezra Pound's admonition to "make it new," I had attended to the *make* and the *new* but not the *it*. Originality—*newness*—as I discovered it to be in "When You Go Away," hybridizes genre convention with individual vision. "When You Go Away" is at once wholly familiar and at home in its conventions and yet wildly strange and disorienting.

How, I had wondered, an undergraduate led to *The Lice* by my teachers Marcia Southwick and Larry Levis (it must have been 1979 or 1980), can one redeem a tired subject? For that is what the lyric convention of "When You Go Away" had seemed to me. The premise of the poem is familiar: when the lover is separated from the beloved, the order of the world changes. Given the limits of that conventional subject, that Poundian "it," how does one make a thing at once faithful to its convention *and* new, recognizable *and* defamiliarized? Then, everywhere I looked, I began to notice wonderful original models of this lyric convention, from the anonymous "Western Wind" to Bob Dylan's "Tomorrow Is a Long Time."

Let's first return to those final lines in "When You Go Away": "my words are the garment of what I shall never be / Like the tucked sleeve of a one-armed boy." In the poem, the lover recalls that he is "the reason," but the reason for what? The beloved's departure and present absence? The lover addresses the absent beloved, but absent, how can he be heard? How can his words, the medium of his art, have agency upon her? His words are a "garment," but what is their function? Do they shelter the body? Do they ornament the body? Do they cloak and conceal the body? Do they wrap and reveal the body? Then the garment metaphor is modified, and while the metaphor becomes more specified by modification, it becomes more various and tangled as well: "my words are the garment of what I shall never be." The speaker's words clothe a future negation, not so much of the beloved's absence, which thus far has been the subject of the poem, but of what the self—the lover—will not achieve. What is that? I do not know, and when I think the next line will answer all the above questions, it instead adds to them.

The metaphor of the word-garment is further modified by a simile: "my words are the garment of what I shall never be / Like the tucked sleeve of a one-armed boy." In what way are his words, which are garments, like the garment that is "the tucked sleeve of a one-armed boy"? Are his words meant to expose or hide a lack? Is the tucked sleeve an image of what fails to fill it—the boy's missing arm? Or is the sleeve, tucked, not dangling, an attempt, as Jennifer Atkinson has pointed out, not to call attention to that which is missing—the phantom limb that feels, but is not, there? These are the sorts of questions I was asking myself thirty years ago when I first came upon the poem and the intricacy of this image. I am still asking them.

One of the possible, and often central, concerns of an art is its own medium. The nature of any auditory or verbal art—and lyric poetry is such an art—is that it rises out of silence, utters sounds, and returns to silence. The poem exists in the instance of its utterance, then is gone until reread or revoiced. In *The Rain in the Trees*, we find it is not so often the beloved who is absent, as in "When You Go Away," but words, the poet's currency, words to give shape to the missing, the lost, and the extinct.

In "Witness," a short four-line poem, Merwin writes:

> I want to tell what the forests
> were like
>
> I will have to speak
> in a forgotten language

The poet faces a double crisis. The only way to communicate the existence of a thing now threatened and on the verge of extinction is a "forgotten" language, perhaps an archaic, obsolete language, a dead language, or a language, like the forest itself, already almost vanished. Another possible reading is that this "forgotten language" is an occult and hermetic language that the poet can speak but few who listen can decipher and understand. Either way, the *witness* of this poem is the articulation of the desire to bear witness. The poem offers a somewhat defeated admission that the words to do so may not wholly communicate. Throughout *The Rain in the Trees*, the poet attempts to wrap language around the central irritant of loss, around the complexity and paradox of absence and its dogged ineffability. The poet hears and knows an arcane language and is burdened to translate it, to witness to those who cannot access and understand it.

In the poem "Utterance," Merwin speaks to the poet's role as a conduit and medium between the ancient and sacred and the present tense of the quotidian and mundane:

> Sitting over words
> very late I have heard a kind of whispered sighing
> not far
> like a night wind in pines or like the sea in the dark
> the echo of everything that has ever
> been spoken
> still spinning its one syllable
> between the earth and silence

Here the absent language must be courted, conjured, by way of words. By "sitting over words" during the late hour, the poet can listen for and hear the "sigh" and "echo of everything that has ever / been spoken." In "Utterance," the manner is mystical, with the poet admitting to a sensitive antenna that can pick up all the frequencies "between earth and silence," between the heard and unheard, as "a single syllable."

Loss is Merwin's subject in *The Rain in the Trees*. The losses range from the intimate to the global, from a personal memory flickering out to the colonial destruction of an indigenous culture to the extinction of whole species. His conventional mode throughout the book is elegiac, but the poems mourn and lament the loss of much more than individual humans, although the loss of his parents, the receding distance of childhood, and a nostalgia for a past home give shape to many poems here. Here his words are not the garments of what he will never be. Instead, he uses language to bridge the gaps between the known and the as-yet-unknown, between what one can articulate and what one has felt, between diurnal and geologic time, between the moment and the mythic, as in "Losing a Language":

> A breath leaves the sentences and does not come back
> yet the old still remember something that they could say
>
> but they know now that such things are no longer believed
> and the young have fewer words
>
> many of the things the words were about
> no longer exist
>
> the noun for standing in mist by a haunted tree
> the verb for I

In an intimate poem, "The First Year," knowledge and language unhinge from one another:

> When the words had all been used
> for other things
> we saw the first day begin
>
> out of the calling water
> and the black branches
> leaves no bigger than your fingertips
> were unfolding on the tree of heaven
> against the old stained wall
> their green sunlight
> that had never shone before
>
> waking together we were the first
> to see them
> and we knew them then
>
> all languages were foreign and the first
> year rose

The speaker and the beloved find gnosis when words have "all been used." Only then does time begin in this Edenic (or is it post-Edenic?) realm. Their insight and knowledge are theirs only in a realm of the ineffable where "all languages" are "foreign."

In a wholly original elegy for John Keats, "Chord," Keats's short life is written as parallel to the ecology and history of Hawai'i at the same moment: "While Keats wrote they were cutting down the sandalwood forests," the poem begins, and it ends with another lamentation for a damaged language and culture:

> while he coughed they carried the trunks to the hole in the forest the
> size of a foreign ship
> while he groaned on the voyage to Italy they fell on the trails and were
> broken
> when he lay with the odes behind him the wood was sold for cannons
> when he lay watching the window they came home and lay down
> and an age arrived when everything was explained in another language

Questions about language riddle Merwin's work. In "Losing a Language," for instance, the loss equals the loss of knowledge, culture, and understanding, while in "The First Year," language must be exhausted and set aside in order to achieve vision and insight. Are we to imagine Keats's short life and small body of work equal to the felling of a sandalwood forest, that the triumph of the language of Keats's poems is somehow implicated in the arrival of an age in Hawai'i "when everything was explained in another language"?

Merwin's poems in *The Rain in the Trees* tend to ask more questions than they answer. They rise out of a silence as if out of an aftermath. Their drama is often offstage, as it was in the first poem I discussed from *The Lice*, where all motivating action is contained in the title "When You Go Away." Or they rely on lyric convention, such as the poem of travel and leave-taking. In "Travelling Together," the conventional subject prepares the reader for the pathos that follows:

> If we are separated I will
> try to wait for you
> on your side of things
>
> your side of the wall and the water
> and of the light moving at its own speed
> even on leaves that we have seen
> I will wait on one side
>
> while a side is there

Here, as in so many of Merwin's poems, the present tense is a precarious place to be. Loss and absence impinge on all sides. The speaker will wait for the absent "you" "on one side," but only "while a side is there." The final line suggests that "a side" could easily vanish, and thus the speaker's waiting would cease. At the same time, one might read the poem's final sentence as an offer to wait forever: walls and water, one could imagine, will always separate this side from that (although unlikely in the eco-poetical world of Merwin's poetry).

As these various examples suggest, *absence*, as a concept, object, and experience, is a constant subject in Merwin's work. Throughout *The Rain in the Trees* one senses a growing anxiety about the continuation of language as a meaning-making tool. Language is as endangered, one could conclude reading these poems, as any of the endangered flora and fauna the book catalogs. I would like to close with the poem "Native Trees," an elegy of sorts for Merwin's parents, written in an austere manner and style wholly different from that of "When You Go Away," the first Merwin poem to wholly enthrall me.

> Neither my father nor my mother knew
> the names of the trees
> where I was born
> what is that
> I asked and my
> father and mother did not
> hear they did not look where I pointed
> surfaces of furniture held
> the attention of their fingers
> and across the room they could watch
> walls they had forgotten
> where there were no questions
> no voices and no shade
>
> Were there trees
> where they were children
> where I had not been
> I asked
> were there trees in those places
> where my father and my mother were born
> and in that time did
> my father and my mother see them
> and when they said yes it meant
> they did not remember
> What were they I asked what were they
> but both my father and my mother
> said they never knew

In "Native Trees," as in so many poems in *The Rain in the Trees*, the loss is potentially permanent and irremediable. In "When You Go Away," the speaker can console himself with the knowledge that "I am the reason," but in "Native Trees," the loss outweighs blame and responsibility. This loss is one of extinction, a wholly severed connection, and the effacement of tribal knowledge.

A Time of Memories
Incorrect but Powerful

Reading *The Rain in the Trees*

Debra Kang Dean

In 1990, one year after I graduated from the University of Montana's MFA program, W. S. Merwin came to Missoula to participate in a conference called "In the Thoreau Tradition." *The Rain in the Trees*[1] had been published two years earlier, and Merwin's letters calling attention to the devastating ecological consequences of geothermic energy development already begun in Wao Kele O Puna, a lowland rain forest on the Big Island of Hawai'i, had appeared in *American Poetry Review*.[2] Although by that time I had lived on the mainland for many years, I was born and raised on the island of O'ahu and had spent a few summers with relatives in Ha'ikū, Maui (Merwin's adopted home since the 1970s). In 1974 I left the islands—for good, I thought—so I was surprised when, in response to the creative thesis that many drafts later became my first book, *News of Home*, a few of my classmates said, "You must be so homesick." It was true, I realized, except that I had also come to recognize that the home I longed for no longer existed; the world of pineapple fields and canneries into which I was born had rapidly given way to tourism. Moreover, what I had felt without understanding or being able to articulate were the pangs of displacement, situated as I was between the influx of Japanese tourists and Filipinos fleeing Ferdinand Marcos's repressive regime and the countervailing pressures of the nascent Second Hawaiian Renaissance.

Fifteen years away from the islands, I had entered into that space of doubt called life-after-the-MFA. I confess that this moment in my writing life and the particular context of Merwin's visit—my late husband was a Thoreau scholar—have enveloped *The Rain in the Trees* in a complex of feelings that has made it my touchstone. As Merwin remarked in an address to the California Academy of Sciences in 1992, "One of the things that's happened in the history of the arts—you see it in moments of great genius, in all the arts—is that suddenly a whole new area of experience lights up. It's possible to see it—whether it's in music or in painting or literature, whatever it is. Suddenly a whole new part of experience becomes available."[3] Indeed, aspects of my experience had once again become available to me because of this book—and a keener sense of the connection and distinction between loss and forgetting, wherein lay for me a renewal of belief in writing as an act both of recovery and of witness. Between regrets about the past and anticipation of the future, I caught glimpses of the elusive present as the self was clarified. Parts of experience that had always been there but obscured by anger and despair, by anxiety and fear, were now *here*. What this kind of awakening looks like Merwin reveals in the contrasting color imagery of the sepia tones of "Print Fallen Out of Somewhere" and the green world of "Tracing the Letters"; in both poems, color is a quality inherent in objects, not the object itself, and points to the perceiver's relationship with the world.

In offering the following reading of some of the poems in *The Rain in the Trees*, I will try to articulate the experience of homecoming that reading that collection represented for one who had spent her formative years in the islands.[4] Symbols, according to *The New Princeton Encyclopedia of Poetry and Poetics*, are "metaphor in reverse,"[5] a slippery definition that has some bearing on my "subjective" reading and also on a more "objective" one. I take this definition to mean that a reader must bring the vehicle to the poem, whose form gives shape to the tenor. One example of a poem operating symbolically rather than metaphorically is Stanley Kunitz's "The Knot," where the full emotional import of the extended symbol emerges if either one knows about the persistence in the poet's life and work of a father's suicide and a mother's response to that event, or, from the poem's formal shape and action, one can bring to bear on the poem a particular set of one's own experiences. In the latter case, I am not speaking of reader-response in the theoretical sense but in terms of a reader's experience in the actual world. "Things do not change; we change," Thoreau wrote in the concluding chapter of *Walden*.[6] This is true of our experience with texts as well and might explain why our encounter with a solidly made text may change over time. Certainly, my reading of *The Rain in the Trees* has continued to deepen.

◆ ◆ ◆

While an MFA student, I had taken an anthropology class on the peoples of the Pacific and, for my course project, did research on the overthrow of the kapu system, a code of conduct, centered on a belief in *mana* or spiritual power, that regulated all aspects of life. That course seems now to have been fortuitous preparation for reading *The Rain in the Trees*, and, in particular, "Chord." One meaning of the word *chord* is "a combination of usually three or more musical tones sounded simultaneously,"[7] and in the poem Merwin brings together the sandalwood trade and Keats's odes— "While Keats wrote they were cutting down the sandalwood forests"— events that did, in fact, occur simultaneously in 1819. Kamehameha I, king of Hawai'i, had died in May 1819; by that same month Keats had written five of his great odes, the sixth to be written that fall. Liholiho, who succeeded Kamehameha I, returned after a six-month absence, a symbolic death, and emerged as Kamehameha II. As his first act, he sat at the women's table, gorged himself, overturned the tables, and then ordered all of the temples destroyed. The following year, American missionaries arrived.

Whereas Kamehameha I had regulated the cutting of sandalwood trees, his successor sold the rights to the chiefs, who then drew their followers away from fishing and farming and into logging the trees, whose fragrant wood was highly prized in China. The Hawaiians, exposed for the first time to diseases like syphilis and cholera, were literally decimated. Thus, with the dismantling of the kapu system and the arrival of the missionaries, "an age arrived when everything was explained in another language." The underlying tone of the poem is reflected in the dissonance between "chord" as sacred sound—the archaic meaning of the word is "string of a musical instrument"[8]—and "cord" as a measure of cut wood; it is the third note sounded alongside the decline of Keats's economic and physical well-being and the destruction of the sandalwood forests, which also destroyed a way of life through which a people had lived close to the land and the sea.

◆ ◆ ◆

Knowing something about this part of Hawaiian history gave me a way of reading the sequence of poems that surround "Chord." In "Hearing the Names of the Valleys," Merwin introduces us to two languages, Hawaiian and English, only the latter of which readers actually hear. In "The Strangers from the Horizon," Merwin writes, "without ever having seen them we knew / without ever having seen us they knew / and we knew they knew each other." I read these ships as metonymic representations of the British and American nations, both of whose presences in the islands remain visible in the state flag. I read "The Strangers from the Horizon" and "Conqueror" as not-quite persona poems; rather, they are echoes of a sort that arise from the words the speaker in "Hearing the Names of the Valleys" can neither comprehend nor grasp. And so Merwin, the son of a Presbyterian minister, has traced the origin of his "people" here.

In "Native," Merwin begins to reestablish his relationship with the islands and its people in the wake of the past. The speaker has constructed a roof of materials at hand—"palm fronds and chicken wire"—to shelter "small native / plants in their plastic pots." Among them will grow 'ohia trees, a photograph of which is on the cover of my paperback copy of the book. We have a taste, I think, of what eluded the speaker in "Hearing the Names of the Valleys," as the seedling and the name "'ohia" simultaneously evoke the trees and their meaning. They are

> filled with red flowers red birds
> water notes flying music
> the shining of the gods

In this space, the Latin name *Metrosideros polymorpha* is written but not spoken. The 'ohia figures largely in the cycle of myths about Pele, goddess of volcanoes, who, in a fit of jealousy over the mortal Lohi'au, destroyed the 'ohia lehua groves sacred to her sister Hi'iaka. When I was a child, it was common to hear that picking a lehua blossom would bring rain; only later did I learn the reason for this belief. The story of 'Ōhi'a and Lehua, from which the tree derives its name, is another story about a love triangle involving Pele; picking the blossom enacts a separation of the lovers who had been reunited as tree and blossom.

Three trees are named in this poem—mango, palm, and 'ohia—and only the 'ohia is endemic to the islands and binds the indigenous people to the land through myth. By using the common names of the other two trees, Merwin grounds the poem in the present, where, in addition to cultivating the seedlings, the speaker takes as his task writing the date on "white plastic labels" and recording "their names in Latin / in the shade of the leaves [he has] put there." Moreover, implicit in the poem is the historical past of pineapple (and before them sugar) plantations:

> [mules] were beaten to go
> straight up the hill
> so that in three years the rain
> had washed all the topsoil
>
> out past sea cliffs

The grandchild of men who emigrated from the Far East in the early part of the twentieth century, I enter the story here. My grandfathers arrived after the overthrow, led primarily by Americans, of the Kingdom of Hawai'i in 1893, and just after the system of contract labor officially ended in 1900, when Hawai'i became a territory of the United States.

In the islands, people speak "pidgin English," which is, more properly, a creole language that developed under the exigencies of business; in fact, the word *pidgin* is said to be a "corruption" of the word *business* by the Chinese tongue. Pidgin English was my first language, one that I had already begun to lose as a child in elementary school, for in school it was stigmatized, disparagingly referred to as "baby English." Even as I understand "Losing a Language" to refer more particularly to the Hawaiian language, these lines from the poem seem true to my felt experience as someone born into pidgin:

> the children will not repeat
> the phrases their parents speak
>
> somebody has persuaded them
> that it is better to say everything differently

> so that they can be admired somewhere
> farther and farther away
>
> . . . .
>
> we are wrong and dark
> in the eyes of the new owners

When I left the islands in 1974, I was ignorant of most of the historical knowledge I have included here; it was taught neither in school nor at home. When we watched the news during those turbulent times, it was at the request of an aunt who had asked that we look out for her son, an infantryman in Vietnam about whom one heard the occasional joke, "I hope he doesn't get mistaken for the enemy."

◆ ◆ ◆

One cannot remember what one doesn't know, and one cannot recover exactly the thing that is lost. Variants of the words *remember* and *forget* frequently recur in *The Rain in the Trees*, and so one takes note of back-to-back titles using variants of the word *loss*. "The Lost Originals" helped me to see with greater clarity my relationship both with language and with the place of my birth and its people. The Hawaiian culture was a preliterate one, and in "Hearing the Names of the Valleys" the speaker encounters a language so different from his own that he can attach no meaning to it—he "cannot remember the sounds." In this light it is easy to understand how the language of a preliterate society can be lost, and to look with new regard on the process of putting words down "on a piece of paper."

Yet "The Lost Originals" is a poem that also asks us to consider language as an instrument of culture. Through the "white plastic labels" and "plastic pots" used with 'ōhia seedlings in "Native," this poem tacitly suggests that the world of the originals cannot be recovered. While we may be grateful for the knowledge available to us through the documents left by missionaries and early converts, the meanings have already been filtered through a Western sensibility and cannot deliver to us the "original" culture as it existed before the Hawaiians had contact with Europeans. This failure of "translation" is implicit in "Kanaloa," in which the god Kanaloa, rather than shown as an oppositional figure like the devil, is restored to his place as a complement to the god Kāne. In "The Lost Originals" we confront the fact that for the Other to survive "as we do," much of the culture embodied by the Other's language will be lost through the very process of assimilation that makes survival possible. A figure like "the old man" in "Hearing the Names of the Valleys," however, is a gateway to another source of knowledge about the lost originals. Through the oral history he commands, he remembers—an act that goes beyond simple recall to retaining and reviving a world—and can thus also call a semblance of that world into being.

This distinction between written history that has left marks on the land and memory closely linked with the oral history that suffers erasure, is at the heart of "Witness," where the speaker says that to be able to "tell what the forests were like," he would have to "speak in a forgotten language." Obviously, such witness is an impossible task in recovering the world now lost, but there is value in trying to save the language and the traces of the world encoded in the words themselves—as *place*holders for what remains. This movement outward toward the Other seems to be an act of faith through which one might begin to believe "in a homeland," and so it is not surprising to find "Place" immediately preceding "Witness." Both planting trees and cultivating a language are activities in the present that are of intrinsic value because they link the past to the future. In "The Biology of Art," Merwin describes the effects of such work as the attainment of a kind of transparency of self, which elsewhere has been named "the verb for I." In "The Archaic Maker," this insight is coupled with an articulation of profound statements about memory and our existence in time:

> In the story it is already tomorrow. A time of memories incorrect but powerful. Outside the window it is the next of everything.
> One of each.
> But here is ancient today
> itself
> the air the living air
> the still water

◆ ◆ ◆

"A time of memories incorrect but powerful"—this is an idea that Merwin previously embodied in "The Houses," first published in his collection of poems *Opening the Hand* (1983).[9] That poem recounts two different occasions when, on a trip to the woods with his father, a son ventures away and upon returning tells his father about a house he has seen. On the first occasion, he is a fairly young child and convinces his father to go with him to the place where he's seen a house but discovers that his father is right: the house is not actually there. On the second occasion, as they are driving away from wooded property his father has purchased, the son, much older now, is again told by his father that there's no house there, and the son ceases to talk about it. After his father's death, the son returns to the place where he'd seen the second house and reflects on the fact that

> the farm is sold and the woods are cut and the subject
> never brought up again but long after the father
> is dead the son sees the two houses

In "Apparitions," the poem that follows "The Houses," the speaker will "see" the father too, thus linking the work of the imagination and of memory with both the natural and the human worlds.

These ideas are recast in "Term," where, in the course of insatiable and perhaps unstoppable development, the speaker says that the meaning of a road will be lost if the road itself is lost, and everyone will be made a foreigner when, as seems inevitable, the road vanishes. However, in the two sides of "what is sacred"—on the one hand, it is another way of saying "Is nothing sacred?" and, on the other, it is an earnest question about the deepest human values—Merwin implies that a choice about the fate of this road might yet be made. I think "Term" is a kind of complement to "Memory," where a choice in the actual world cannot be made. Here is that poem in full:

> Climbing through a dark shower
> I came to the edge of the mountain
>
> I was a child
> and everything was there
>
> the flight of eagles the passage of warriors
> watching the valley far below
>
> the wind on the cliff the cold rain blowing upward
> from the rock face

everything around me had burned
and I was coming back

walking on charcoal among the low green bushes
wet on the skin and wide awake

If read autobiographically—and statements Merwin has made would invite us to do so[10]—the reference to childhood in "Memory" locates the setting in Pennsylvania. The actual landscape of childhood has been lost, but not entirely; the powerful charge of memory and "the low green bushes" bear it into the future.

The context of the book in which "Memory" appears invites me to link its "low green bushes" with the stubborn persistence of the 'ohia on lava land so that I see, as it were, two landscapes in an instant. Because Merwin has drawn within the sphere of eternity two points of our history's dark line, one can, wherever one stands, mark other points on that same line in a world that seems hell-bent on material progress. For this reason, twenty-one years after I first read *The Rain in the Trees*, I still believe that not only will it remain a book "full of words important to remember," but that it will also afford an encounter that holds the possibility of awakening readers into "the world of the living"—while there is still time. When asked why he wrote poems, Robert Frost is said to have answered, "For the lark!"[11] *The Rain in the Trees* inspires in me that same multidimensional answer. Through a vision of palm fronds, chicken wire, and plastic labels and pots, Merwin reveals the layers of time in what is now here.

Merwin's Evolving Protocols

On the Occasion of "The Day Itself"

Steven Cramer

> *Occasional poetry is the highest kind.*
> —Goethe[1]

In his preface to *The Second Four Books of Poems* (1993),[2] W. S. Merwin attributes his relinquishment of punctuation in the mid-1960s to his "growing sense that punctuation alluded to and assumed an allegiance to the rational protocol of written language . . . I had come to feel that it stapled the poems to the page." His metaphor suggests linguistic custom pinning down "the viewless wings of poesy," the way a lepidopterist fixes specimens to a mounting board. Unpunctuated writing, in this view, liberates speech by releasing poetic energies suppressed by convention. Roughly fifty years have elapsed since a question mark—concluding "The Crossroads of the World Etc." from *The Moving Target* (1963)—served as Merwin's parting shot to punctuation.[3] Debates regarding the wisdom of his persistence in banishing it from his work hit an impasse long ago: "Keep the lost garment," goes his last punctuated sentence, "where would I find the owner?"

It's the dynamic of Merwin's "allegiance to the rational protocol of written language" that I want to explore here: specifically, how dramatically his sensibility has evolved toward a rapprochement with those behavioral codes—of language and of cultural tradition generally. The tipping point of this transformation seems to me the 1993 volume *Travels*,[4] in which a more nuanced attitude toward convention finds its most persuasive expression, appropriately enough in a commissioned work, "The Day Itself." Published in *Travels* but unveiled five years earlier, on June 4, 1989, as the Harvard

Phi Beta Kappa poem, "The Day Itself" endorses, with graceful tact (and plenty of caveats), the quintessential ceremony that observes "the wisdom of the tribe" as it passes from generation to generation. The poem constitutes a major advance in Merwin's work—not despite but *because* of its performance as an occasional poem, fully, if skeptically, occupied with the protocols of its occasion.

It's a critical commonplace to assign middle-period Merwin charter membership in the Deep Imagist faction of poets of the 1960s and 1970s, for whom the literary etiquette inherited from earlier decades was inimical to their poetic stimulus plan. According to this school, the sources of human psychology lay beneath the socialized ego, so poetry discovered its true sustenance, and its emancipation, in a reservoir of collective archetypes. Paul Breslin's *The Psycho-political Muse: American Poetry since the Fifties* (1987), a mostly unfriendly position paper on the midcentury poetic zeitgeist, summarized Deep Imagism's aesthetic ideology: "What all these formulations have in common is their location of the sacred or the authentic in some extremely 'deep' layer of consciousness that lies at the other extreme from language, culture, and conscious thought, at the point where we are connected to unconscious animal nature or even to inanimate nature."[5] Breslin singles out Merwin's poetry as the most extreme in its withdrawal from the impure products of civilization: "in most of his poems from *The Moving Target* through *Writings to an Unfinished Accompaniment* (1973), Merwin has tried to work in a voluntary blindness, without any of the usual windows that lyric poetry opens from the inwardness of feeling to its historical sources in the external world."[6]

Culture, history, circumstance, identifiable locations: middle-period Merwin not only expunges these from his poetry but presupposes their extinction. The opening poem from *The Lice* (1967)[7] presents a characteristic postapocalyptic mindscape:

The Animals

All these years behind windows
With blind crosses sweeping the tables

And myself tracking over empty ground
Animals I never saw

I with no voice

Remembering names to invent for them
Will any come back will one

Saying yes

Saying look carefully yes
We will meet again

The epitome of Merwin's Deep Imagist idiom, "The Animals" seems not so much written as pieced together from shreds of ancient parchment, offering no anchoring punctuation or syntax, no plot or argument. Plural nouns make for a field of reference that blurs the more we try to focus. What passes for concrete detail—"blind crosses sweeping the tables" evoking, however faintly, the shadows of window sashes—doesn't coalesce into reliable denotation. The setting, such as it is, shifts in line 3 to an outdoor "ground" notable only for its emptiness. The speaker tracks animals he's never seen, for reasons we can't discern. To posit a "speaker" in the first place—after all, he's mute—overlooks just how completely this poem is struck dumb.

And yet "The Animals" does pick through a few leftovers of cultural reference. "Blind crosses" connote the remnants of sacred icons, their visionary power long since extinguished. The remembered/invented names dimly call to mind an Eden existing before universal deforestation. Moreover, a skeletal semantic "plot" shifts the emotional charge from negative (*blind / empty / never / no*) to positive (*remembering / invent / yes / meet*). I read the final line as the completion of an urgent question, begun in line 7—"not likely" the implied answer. The line itself might echo the time-worn anthem of wartime consolation: *We'll meet again, don't know where, don't know when. . . .* If so, Merwin samples it here in much the way Stanley Kubrick does to conclude *Dr. Strangelove*. The poem's total effect offers no assurance that the animals will return, affirm, or give counsel; or that inarticulate humanity's pursuit will relieve its yearning. "The Animals" indexes the disillusioned axioms of Merwin's middle period: traditional symbols lack consequence; the human animal has orphaned itself from its kin; and civilization's supreme invention, language, weakly recalls its power to invent.

For the next twenty-five years, although occasionally less dispiritedly and progressively more autobiographically, Merwin continues to portray social progress as the cause of nature's extinction. By *The Rain in the Trees* (1988),[8] humankind's shock and awe campaign is doubly murderous. Along with obliterating the environment, it wipes out the native vitality of language. Its power to store memory, rescue belief, and name with precision is reduced to collateral damage:

> A breath leaves the sentences and does not come back
> yet the old still remember something that they could say
>
> but they know now that such things are no longer believed
> and the young have fewer words
>
> many of the things the words were about
> no longer exist
>
> the noun for standing in mist by a haunted tree
> the verb for I
>
> the children will not repeat
> the phrases their parents speak
>
> somebody has persuaded them
> that it is better to say everything differently
>
> so that they can be admired somewhere
> farther and farther away
>
> where nothing that is here is known
> we have little to say to each other

There's a hint of the grumpy dad here, badgering his kids to go play outside, where a tree really used to *be* something. Of course, the children are part of the collateral damage, deprived of linguistic access to their heritage by the same predatory forces that despoil the environment. But their own willfulness, gullibility, and susceptibility to ego gratification collaborate in the seduction to embrace newfangled ways of saying. The countercultural poet appears to have aged into a bit of a scold, albeit an empathic one.

Merwin's ambivalence shows most richly when "Losing a Language" is read in conjunction with its near neighbors in the book, including "Hearing the Valleys," "Conqueror," "Native," "Chord," and "The Lost Originals." No less anguished about the "shamelessness of men" for whom "everything [is] theirs because they thought so,"[9] by the time of *The Rain in the Trees* Merwin has become a good deal more self-implicating (see especially "Hearing the Names of the Valleys"), as well as more down-to-earth. The voiceless ones in poems such as "The Animals"—seeking, over denuded landscapes, animals they never saw—registered as literary emblems. In Hawai'i in 1988, to lose a language is to sever flesh-and-blood communities from their cultural roots.

But is "the conqueror" our *use* of language in bad faith or language itself, intrinsically false because inherently fabricated? In a 1988 interview, Merwin contends that "[naming] sets up a concept between you and the thing you are looking at. The cat doesn't know it's a cat until you teach it that it is a cat."[10] One could debate the odds of teaching a cat self-knowledge, but Merwin's truism is true enough. If language always sets up barriers between perceiver and perceived, why not give silence the last word? The answer is as obvious as it is unhelpful: improving on the blank page is Item One in the writer's job description. Words never *equal* "the thing you are looking at"; at best they approximate, through analogy, the speechless world our senses apprehend. Despite its overtly political content, "Losing a Language" implies that having "little to say to each other" constitutes a tragic human universality.

Precisely because it rediscovers a multiplicity of ways we can "say to each other," *Travels* seems to me Merwin's most surprising book since *The Lice*. He takes on personas, historical and invented, in three dramatic monologues. He compresses biography into crisp storytelling in "Rimbaud's Piano," a poignant recounting of the *poète maudit's* last years. He renews a conversation with received forms, as in the pitch-perfect rhymed tetrameters of "Search Party." Most bracingly, he revitalizes his interest in, and genius for, the orchestration of tone. In the space of a few syllables, the book's prologue poem, "Cover Note," replaces Baudelaire's notorious sneer with a circumspect appeal to the reader:

> Hypocrite reader my
> variant my almost
> family we are so
> few now it seems as though
> we knew each other as
> the words between us keep
> assuming that we do
> I hope I make sense to
> you

Adopted voices, subject matter rooted in historical events and personages (*Travels* is the first Merwin collection to include endnotes), and reengagement with formal symmetries rejuvenate Merwin's poetry. Turning outward from solipsism, he becomes more sanguine about the human community's potential to sustain itself. In short, he rediscovers an audience, literally so in "The Day Itself," the book's most public and most hospitable poem, written at least five years before the publication of *Travels*, so perhaps a catalyst for this breakthrough.

Deliberately official, "The Day Itself" unwinds with a stately rhetorical authority that Merwin had previously shunned. I happened to be in the audience the day Merwin "delivered" his commissioned work, and of course heard the resonant one-word refrain, "know." The poem's rhymes and off-rhymes (*aabbbba* in the first and last stanzas, otherwise predominantly *aabbcca*), the syllabic pattern in its eighteen seven-line stanzas, and its organization into five "movements"—those registered, if at all, subliminally. Depending how liberally or conservatively the reader interpolates punctuation—especially the semicolon—four of the five movements constitute a single sentence. The inarguable exception, the last movement, employs shorter syntactical units to powerful effect, as we will hear.

The first movement (stanzas 1 through 5) opens with a gentle joke, tweaking the occasion even as it sets in motion a qualified ode to the values of culturally acquired knowledge—in short, a college education:

> Now that you know
> everything does it not come even so
> with a breath of surprise the particular
> awaited morning in summer

when the leaves that you walked under
since you saw them unfold out of nothing whether
you noticed that or not into

the world you know
have attained the exact weave of shadow
they were to have and the unrepeatable
length of that water which you call
The Charles the whole way to its end
has reached the bridge at last after descending and
gathering its own color through

all that you know
and is slipping under the arches now
while the levelled ground embraced by its famous
facades the ordinary place
where you were uncertain
late moonstruck cold angry able to imagine
you had it all to yourself to

use and to know
without thinking much about it as though
it were the real you suddenly shines before
you transformed into another
person it seems by the presence
of familiar faces all assembled at once
and a crowd of others you do

not really know
rippling in the shimmer of daylight row
upon row sending up a ceaseless leafy
shuffle of voices out of the
current that is rushing over
the field of common chairs one of them opened here
at the moment only for you

Severely edited, stripped of its lithe syntax, tonal agility, and playful wit, this thirty-five-line Socratic question condenses to this kernel: *Now that you know everything, does it not come with a surprise* [on this] *morning when the leaves have attained the shadow they were to have, and the Charles has reached the bridge and is slipping under the arches, while the leveled ground shines before you* [who are] *transformed by the familiar faces assembled and the voices rushing over common chairs, one* [of which is] *opened for you?*

Restoring subordination to the core sentence shows how rigorously Merwin deploys his elaborations and how fully the protocols he discredited now receive their due. Like the summer leaves' "exact weave of shadow," analogies branch out to both enact and parse the poem's subject. "Breath" inaugurates a series of images that hold nature and culture in equilibrium, distinct yet interdependent. The morning promises a noteworthy communal event; leaves unfold to shade the procession; the ground ("leveled," presumably, by Harvard's Physical Plant department) accepts the "embrace" of façades that border the yard; the river, unrepeatable yet named, retains its own color but interacts with the bridges and arches; the moon presides over a spectrum of human feeling; light dapples the seating formation; and, most beautifully, the audience's murmur of anticipation registers as a "ceaseless leafy / shuffle."

The rhymes and off-rhymes (often encapsulations of content: *shadow / unrepeatable; end / and; uncertain / imagine*) support the sensory and syntactical patterns as a soundtrack does its film. In a gradual tightening of perspective, the movement first takes in the city, the river, and the campus (with a brief flashback to moony passions familiar to any undergraduate), then pans across the "field" of temporary seating to focus, finally, on one among the hundreds of "common chairs" reserved "only for you." In a brilliant superimposition, the poem conflates the singular and the plural second-person viewpoint, so that "you" always represents both a single graduate and the entire graduating class. There's an equally intricate montage of tenses created by the verbs, participles, and temporal transitions: *Now; walked; since; has reached; after; is slipping; were; suddenly shines; assembled at once; is rushing; opened here / at the moment.* Like Whitman, Merwin unites past and present as he addresses the one as many, the many as one.

Mapping the occurrences of "know" discloses the amplitude of the poem's erudition about learning. The opening joke links knowledge and revelation; in stanza 2, the known world's "weave of shadow" identifies knowledge with the senses; stanza 3 likens knowledge's transience to river flow; stanza 4 gently critiques youth's tendency to know thoughtlessly; stanza 5 introduces the interplay of knowing and unknowing, central to the poem's development.

The second movement (approximately stanzas 8 through 9, constituting four sentences or one, depending on how one mentally punctuates certain junctures) shifts from interrogative to imperative voice. Merwin turns avuncular as he reminds the graduates that learning is rooted in self-knowledge. Appropriately, he begins with an allusion to Western philosophy's earliest advocates for introspection:

> and you should know
> who that [i.e., yourself] is as the man some time ago
> in Greece you remember is supposed to have
> said and there was that other of
> his countrymen about whom we
> are certain of little who was sure already
> without having met you that you
>
> could get to know
> you whoever that is if you were so
> inclined

I suppose "the man some time ago / in Greece" to be Plato, and that hazy "other of / his countrymen" to be his teacher Socrates, or perhaps the even more shadowy pre-Socratic Pythagoras, to whom the inscription over the entrance to the temple at Delphi—"Man know thyself; then thou shalt know the Universe and God"—is attributed. In any case, Merwin pays guarded homage to what Western philosophical tradition is "supposed to have said." And just as "we are certain of so little" about who these first philosophers were, our own identities amount to a vague "whoever." Merwin devotes the rest of the second movement to playing a set of variations on the tautologies and paradoxes that complicate the tradition's central precept, *know thyself*. His wit shows best in discrete extracts:

> perhaps you do
>
> not in fact know
> you in the first place but might have to go
> looking for you when here you are after all . . .
>
> behind your
> own face now is the you that you
>
> wanted to know . . .
>
> [you] are the same you that you were
> as long as you can remember . . .

If you want to find yourself, there you are, goes the old gnomic joke, but that's too glib to do justice to Merwin's sophisticated, but never sophistic, lecture. In his earlier work, binary thinking posed Dionysian id-energy against Apollonian ego-reflection, the archaic vigor of the former colonized by the rational imperialism of the latter. The author of "The Day Itself" constructs a much more prismatic model of psychology.

Similarly Athenian, the poem's third movement (most of stanza 10 through two lines of stanza 12, indisputably a single sentence) reflects on choice and chance, and the tension between them that eludes either wish or will. A breathtaking dissolve inaugurates this movement, Merwin's audience first taken back to before their births and then elevated into the cosmos:

> furthermore
> what influenced each of your
> choices all of the accidents
> as they are called and such chances as your parents'
> meeting on their own before you
>
> were here to know
> where you were coming from those joys with no
> histories those crimes painted out those journeys
> without names the flawless courses
> of all the stars the progression
> of the elements were moving in unison
> from what you had never seen to

what you now know
you were so long looking forward to . . .

Again it helps to distill the nuclear sentence: *What influenced your choices (accidents, chances, joys, crimes, and the courses of stars and elements) moved you from what you had never seen to what you now know you were looking forward to.* In paraphrase, this is familiar territory—fate equals character; character, fate—but the supple phrasing, subtle rhymes, and suggestive asides vivify notions as least as old as Periclean Athens.

Merwin veers most closely to his 1960s complaint against inherited ways of knowing in the penultimate movement (stanzas 12 through 16, approximately). Unlike the middle-period poetry, however, these stanzas don't indict "book learning" per se. Rather, they take time out to acknowledge knowledge, as it were—skeptically but not dismissively. Merwin's richly complicated manner—by turns funny, sober, offhand—makes for one of the poem's most disarmingly matter-of-fact excursions. "[N]o / wonder [what you've learned] floats before you appearing at / once inevitable and not / yet there," the movement's single sentence begins—again showing Merwin's renewed ingenuity: the pun on "no" and "know" and careful enjambment embedding line meanings within sentence meanings. "[W]hat you must know / by now about knowledge" then undergoes a meticulous risk-benefit analysis, a colon demarcating its preamble from a series of examples divided by four semicolons (my proposed punctuation in brackets):

it also
is a body of questions in apparent
suspension and no different
from the rest of the dream save that
we think we can grasp it and it tends to repeat
itself like the world we wake through

while as you know
it has its limits[:] it belongs to no
one[;] it cannot bring you love or keep you from
catching cold from tomorrow from
loss or waiting[;] it can stand in
its own way so that however you stare you can
not see things about it that you

do in fact know
perfectly well the whole time and can so
loom that you cannot look past it which is more
important[;] you have to acquire
it for yourself but for that you need
gifts and words of others and places set aside
in large part for informing you

until you know
all this which of course may render you no
kinder or more generous since that is not
its function or at least not right
away and may not only make
you no wiser but make it sound wiser to mock
the notions of wisdom since you

have come to know
better and in some cases it can go
to your head and stay there[.]

Lecturer and student have begun to merge into an interactive thought process, as concessionary locutions—stock items from the orator's tool-kit—make plain: *as you know*; *you do in fact know perfectly well*; *of course*; *you // have come to know better*. Merwin *and* his audience recognize that knowledge is questionable, provisional, redundant, limited, in the public domain, obstructive, personal, inherited, morally neutral, and can be used stupidly, denigrating its better half, sagacity, because knowledge cannot match wits with it: in those "cases when it can go / to your head and stay there," knowledge without wisdom incapacitates our good natures.

Given how knowledge condones and even fortifies bad faith, can it be used wisely? The poem's fifth and final movement offers no answer. Instead, four relatively terse sentences don't so much recognize its value as concede, a little reluctantly, that we value it.[11] The new clipped rhythm distinguishes the movement from the previous four, signaling its function as the lecture's *peroratio* (my proposed punctuation again in brackets):

yet we are here
to speak well of it[.] we treasure

70

something about it or we say
we do beyond the prospect of making money
and so on with it[.] something you

certainly know
of it that has led to its being so
often compared to the light which you see all
around you at the moment full
of breath and beginnings[.] how well
you know what that is and soon you will start to tell
us and we will listen to you

For all of its flaws, then, we are often moved to gather in praise of learn-ing (one can picture Merwin prepping for "The Day Itself" by rereading Antony's speech to the Roman plebeians). Does Merwin himself have *any-thing* good to say about it? I think so. Used well, understood, its tendency toward acquisitiveness checked, knowledge can clarify the past and help illuminate the future. More important, like the light it is said to be like, it can widen our perspectives on the present. *Most* important, it forms a crucial link between generations. Merwin reinforces that link by assem-bling six first-person plural pronouns in these last twelve lines ("we" appeared only four times previously, none referring to the gathering at hand). Recapitulating the image of breath that inspired the poem's open-ing, and substituting "the light which you all / see around you" for the "exact weave of shadow" from stanza 2, Merwin invites his audience, his readers, and himself into a jointly imagined preview of the future, when the graduates will deliver the speeches. In a little structural miracle evident only when one takes an aerial view of the poem, the opening noun clause ("Now that you know") joins with the closing assertion ("we will listen to you") to condense all five movements into a single, encompassing sentence. Scansion helps us hear its cadence: "*Nów* that you *knów, wé* will *lís*ten to *yóu.*" In a way, Merwin makes no claims for the value of knowledge; only his language does.

Unapologetically didactic, slyly Socratic in its rhetorical tactics, making use of traditional prosody to buttress a rigorously constructed argument, "The Day Itself" behaves like a good instructor (from the Latin *instructio-nem:* building, arrangement, teaching). How far Merwin's sensibility has come from that of his 1960s and 1970s work can be appreciated when one considers the poem's final gesture—a prediction that presupposes a future from which to reflect back—in the light of Laurence Lieberman's assessment of *The Lice* in *The Yale Review:* "If there is any book that has perfectly captured . . . the agony of a generation that *knows* [my italics] itself to be the last . . . it is W. S. Merwin's *The Lice.*"[12] "The Day Itself" outstrips the complacent nihilism Lieberman singles out for (rather overheated) praise, and forcefully answers Breslin's (rather too broad) critique of the shallow psychologies of Merwin's Deep Imagism.[13] The poet who once saw language "as something to be rescued from public debasement, even wrested from its undeniably public status as something culturally shared,"[14] and who turned away from even "the vestiges . . . of a determinate occasion,"[15] marshals his verbal resources to address a communal ceremony in an occasional poem, one of his most durable.

The Act Finds the Utterance

W. S. Merwin's "Substance"

Forrest Gander

Substance

I could see that there was a kind of distance lighted
    behind the face of that time in its very days as
they appeared to me but I could not think of any
    words that spoke of it truly nor point to anything
except what was there at the moment it was beginning
    to be gone and certainly it could not have been proven
nor held however I might reach toward it touching
    the warm lichens the features of the stones the skin of
the river and I could tell then that it was
    the animals themselves that were the weight and place of
the hour as it happened and that the mass of the cow's neck
    the flash of the swallow the trout's flutter were where it
was coming to pass they were bearing the sense of it
    without questions through the speechless cloud of light

The cover of W. S. Merwin's 1996 collection *The Vixen*[1] is memorably hand-some. His style was changing again, changing but still recognizably his own, that voice uncounterfeitably Merwin's. Other poems light the way to page 56, to the poem called "Substance." Do you remember the way, the landscape of this book?

There are walnut trees along the road. It is southern France, stalks whispering under the bellies of sheep "in crumbling pastures fenced with cut brush." In a little village, the door to a cottage stands "open onto the stone sill smoothed to water," and through the west window, its casement edged with ivy, we can hear at various times swallows, warblers, wrens, crows, a badger; sometimes at night, the bark of a fox.

It is a landscape of trees and rocks, of what the Japanese call "borrowed scenery," one irregular phalanx of green behind another; plants, people, and animals living together, and their shadows lengthening into darkness, but not finally, not into a final darkness, because the syntax of duration here doesn't stop and the syntax of place preserves each thing in a web of interconnectedness, an ongoing relationship. Correspondingly, the poem is a single restless and unpunctuated run-on sentence.

The poem is also a sonnet, and its shape itself a borrowed landscape through which we see a history of the sonnet, updated by Merwin into blank verse but connected by its loose Alexandrines to sonnets written in France by Pierre de Ronsard and Joachim du Bellay. So the poem's very form becomes an expression of both continuity and change, a vision within which we glimpse the flicker of a vision from an earlier era, "a kind of distance lighted." As though to indicate the backward and forward motion of the poem's time, the line itself steps in from and returns repeatedly to the left margin.

And as we read the body of this sonnet, revealed to us between the "lighted" and "light" of the poem's first and last words, we are called toward that earlier time by a subtle, erotic shift of vowels. One assonantal scarf is removed to reveal another, held closer to the French form. The brash, long *i*'s in *I, kind, lighted, behind,* and *time* gradually give way to the soft diphthongs *hour, cow, swallow, trout, without,* and *cloud.*

Remarkably, the poem's syntax and punctuation, its structure, and its shifting vowels all enact the meaning of the poem, all intensify the theme expressed by the lyric speaker, who seems to be trying to trace some line of connection between the past, "a kind of distance lighted," and the present, "what was there at the moment it was beginning / to be gone."

What the speaker finds tenuously touching present to past, what he realizes makes up the substance of the place he loves, is the nonhuman, "the animals themselves." People think they are more than grass, Merwin writes elsewhere, echoing the biblical Isaiah. We imprint the world with our idea of order and time, we articulate the experience of being with our questions and contentions, but our insistence on seeing history as the march of ourselves, the very thought that what we feel might need to be "proven," testifies to our sad limitations. The animals, the speaker realizes, unlike us, bear the sense of the world "without questions through the speechless cloud of light."

Cloud of light: the imagery calls to mind St. John of the Cross. Do you remember? It was he who wrote, "It is a dark cloud that illuminates the night." Often we find in Merwin's poems a trace of his own history as the son of a minister, a child laved by the word of God. We see that history too in his perception of duration as the yoking of location and time. Merwin's poem goes out like a beam of light on a perfect diagonal between the axes of space and time, a vector that the King James Bible beautifully suggests as "the space of an hour." In "Substance," distance, a spatial realm, is located within time, "behind the face of that time in its very days." In fact, the true substance that the poem finally asserts, its mass—"the mass of the cow's neck"—significantly constitutes a form of time, "the weight and place / of the hour."

By insisting that time and place are part and parcel, Merwin's poem asks us to see the world with an expanded imagination of our circumscribed place in it. "Substance" reminds us that we are not the logical arbiters of time's value and substance's extent. Nor is the landscape external to us; it writes meaning into us even as we read meaning into it. The speaker of "Substance" struggles to perceive a world where animals and landscape go on, but he will not go on. However he "might reach toward it touching / the warm lichens the features of the stones," he cannot absorb the world nor make his own attributes coincide with those of time, for it is he himself who is contained by the world in time. If the poem intimates the speaker's mortality, it likewise inspires in him a humility toward it.

Humility because the speaker, like the syntax, like the poem's meaning, is held in abeyance. Merwin's incomparably numinous tone, his merging of time and space, his employment seven times in fourteen lines of the pronoun "it," the paired th's, the gentle assonance in reach / features, weight / place, where / bearing, and the sequence of prepositional relations—distance *behind* the face *of* time *in* days *as* they appeared—expand the outlines of the poem's concerns and limit the sway of our logical determinacy. As we read the poem, we are not always sure what is meant, to what the pronouns refer. It is as though we have entered a larger vocabulary of being. Abstractions and particularities, the speaker's curiosity and the trout's flutter, blur together in a generous enactment of the book of Ephesians' assurance that "we are members of one another." Not just "we" the humans, but "we"—all of it, everything.

And yet might it be argued that "Substance" naively champions a "speechless" world with a masterfully accomplished poetic speech? Do the message and the medium necessarily constitute a self-serving Romantic paradox? Isn't Merwin simply relating to us, much as Wordsworth does, the sermons he himself imparts to the stones?

Says Sophocles, "The man who maintains that only he has the power to reason correctly, the gift to speak, the soul—a man like that, when you know him, turns out empty." Merwin might recast the subject of Sophocles's sentence as "Those who think only their species has the right to speak, the gift, etc." Given the restrictions of our inescapable subjectivity, our translations of the world are always presumptuous, corrupt, and absolutely necessary. Truth and art are interpretations, and all that we call meaning derives from a collaboration between the outer world and inner experience. As an insurance executive once noted, "the blackbird is involved / In what I know." Who are we to sate ourselves on solipsism?

Merwin isn't advocating that we align ourselves with rocks and plants in a primordial, inhuman stupidity. Nor is he sentimentalizing a paradise swept free of human intruders. Despite a long body of work in which he has given shape to his belief that other beings and things are conjoined in the structure of human selfhood, it is finally the quality of Merwin's language that most emphatically advocates for a human place in the world. In "Substance," his syntax renews a plurality; it becomes the organ of a less ego-centered, less logic-driven perception. Here, as elsewhere, Merwin's poetics express the possibilities of a deep investment in attentiveness; they disclose a quality of awareness through which we might imagine the potential of our lives in the world among others—human and not human—who call forth our responsibility as ethical beings.

Most of the Stories Have to Do with Vanishing

Matthew Zapruder

I first read W. S. Merwin's *The Vixen* (1996) in a contemporary poetry course taught by James Tate at the University of Massachusetts at Amherst, where I was a graduate student in the MFA program in poetry.[1] It was either spring or fall, I believe, of 1998. I have, associated with this book, a memory of sad, warm days, but I'm not sure.

I loved being an MFA student, although, without realizing it, I was very unhappy all the time. I read poetry constantly and was writing all sorts of poems (on a manual typewriter that used to belong to my mother in high school, which I had salvaged from my grandparents' attic), all of them failures. I was lucky enough to have Tate, and Dara Wier, and the late, amazing Agha Shahid Ali as teachers. All three were calm in their behavior while being unpredictable in their interests, and all three were writing with great force and power.

My fellow students were bright and nervous, and we all had the sense that something very important was starting to happen, even if we didn't know exactly what it was. It's probably hard to imagine now, but at the time we barely thought about publishing in magazines, much less a book. Of course we wanted to, but that was really for "later." Hardly any of us had published anything, and almost everything we wrote we shared with each other and then changed or threw away or reused for some other purpose. We thought of ourselves as experimenters, practicers, apprentices.

My paperback copy of *The Vixen* is a very light tan color, with what looks like a painting of a fox on the cover. Actually, it's a not a painting or drawing but a blurry, impressionistic photograph, by Minoru Taketazu, presumably from his book *Fox Family: The Four Seasons of Animal Life*, described on Amazon.com with the following irresistible, tragic synopsis: "The life cycle of the Ezo fox, native to the northern islands of Japan, is captured in a photographic essay that follows the fox through the icy winter and birth of cubs in the spring to the family break-up in the fall."

When I open *The Vixen*, I see it's a first edition. I'm sure I must have bought it right when it first came out in paperback, at Wooton's, a small bookstore on the main drag in Amherst where we would go almost every day to lurk and see who else would come in to hang out. That store no longer exists, though its former proprietor, Mark Wooton, is one of the co-owners of the marvelous Amherst Books, right around the corner.

On the first blank page before the title page, in pencil I see written in my handwriting:

- Wed 23 11:30
- Tue 29 2:00
- Wed 30 11:30

and it takes me just a few seconds to realize these are reminders of times I was scheduled to meet my new analyst, with whom I still, all these years later, sometimes speak (on the phone now from California).

At that time, my unhappiness, which I had always just taken for granted, had recently taken on the particularly virulent, malevolent, self-destructive form of a triangular love affair, composed of me and two of my fellow graduate students, a very recent former couple. The whole affair was typical and destructive and inexcusable and humiliating and just generally a giant psychologically inevitable train wreck. All the time I was trying to write poems, and I remember being frustrated, in a poetic sense as well as a personal one. Looking back on it now I can see, with a little tolerance and forgiveness, that I was just starting to understand the possibilities of language as material, in the same way a painter might start at some early point to truly begin to know paint. But at the time I was deep in the middle of many interrelated crises of confidence and couldn't see any way forward, except to thrash wildly in one aesthetic direction or another, in the hope that something would stick.

Some of my difficulties were inherent to the condition of being a novice. Some, however, were a result of the times. In the late 1990s it was taken for granted, widely in poetry and especially in many of the top graduate programs in creative writing, that it was unsophisticated, retrograde, even manipulative to sully whatever was "poetic" in the poem with any kind of story or situation. Everyone knew that a poet had to relinquish the crutch of narrative in order to write true poetry, and not its mere, sad cousin, lyrical prose. "Narrative" applied to a poem was just a euphemism for square, unsophisticated, sappy, self-absorbed, and old-fashioned.

It was therefore a silent article of faith among the students (though not the professors) that any sort of anecdotal narration was by its nature incompatible with poetry. Of course, even a cursory study of poetry from virtually any period would quickly reveal this aesthetic position to be patently incorrect. Yet this was an idea nestled firmly in the minds of many young poets at the time, including my friends and me.

When I think back on it now, I remember this rejection of narrative was also bound up in an idea about who had the "right" to speak. At all costs we wanted to avoid the possibility of being caught out as writers who took on, unintentionally or otherwise, oracular, superior stances that made it seem as if we thought we were better than our readers.

Surely it was good and right that we were questioning the role of the speaker in poems. There had been decades at least of American poetry that had time and again fallen into what Keats called Wordsworth's "egotistical sublime," an ostensible celebration of nature, or the world, that was really about praising the poet's own superior qualities of perceptiveness. We still see this today in those awful, familiar poems where someone goes for a walk in the woods or to a hospital to visit a sick loved one, only to see something beautiful and terrible that reveals the so-called truth of our existence. These poems have the not-so-secret agenda of holding the sensitivity and emotional depth of the poet (and by extension the reader, who is wise and thoughtful and cultured and emotionally advanced enough to be experiencing this marvelous poem) up for our collective admiration.

What we didn't realize was that this stance of the egotistical sublime, however odious, was not inherently related to a use of narrative in poetry. What we wanted was beauty that obliterated all other consideration, lyricism, that singing that can happen only in poetry. And it was right for us to want that. But as beginners in the art, we didn't realize how incredibly difficult it would be to take the rigid and unnecessary stance that narrative could by its very nature not coexist with the lyric.

The mood of *The Vixen* is elegiac, mysterious, historical. Centuries can go by in a few lines, and in many of the poems a cyclical, prehistorical time can interpermeate our modern era. The speaker has bought an old house somewhere in rural France. He walks and meets people, some of whom seem like ghosts from a different, ancient time. Something in his life is ending ("this time / was a time of ending this time the long marriage was over / the orbits were flying apart"), and there are symbolic echoes of this, not too heavy-handed but definitely present in the condition of the old house, which must be rebuilt, as well as in the reappearance of a female fox, the vixen, in real and mythic ways. On his walks the narrator encounters various inhabitants of the rural area. Some of the poems are dreams, some are general meditations on the time of the narrator's life, and some take place in a much older, sometimes medieval, sometimes mythic time.

The Vixen begins with a three-page poem, "Fox Sleep." Like an overture, in its five sections the poem moves through the various times and modes of consciousness that will appear in the rest of the poems of the book. The form of "Fox Sleep" is the same as that of all the rest of the poems in the book: long lines that extend almost to the right margin, every other line indented, no punctuation:

> On a road through the mountains with a friend many years ago
> > I came to a curve on a slope where a clear stream
> flowed down flashing across dark rocks through its own
> > echoes that could neither be caught nor forgotten
> it was the turning of autumn and already
> > the mornings were cold with ragged clouds in the hollows
> long after sunrise but the pasture sagging like a roof
> > the glassy water and flickering yellow leaves
> in the few poplars and knotted plum trees were held up
> > in a handful of sunlight that made the slates on the silent

mill by the stream glisten white above their ruin
    and a few relics of the life before had been arranged
in front of the open mill house to wait
    pale in the daylight out on the open mountain
after whatever they had been made for was over
    the dew was drying on them and there were few who took that road
who might buy one of them and take it away somewhere
    to be unusual to be the only one
to become unknown a wooden bed stood there on rocks
    a cradle the color of dust a cracked oil jar iron pots
wooden wheels iron wheels stone wheels the tall box of a clock
    and among them a ring of white stone the size of an
embrace set into another of the same size
    an iron spike rising from the ring where the wooden
handle had fitted that turned it in its days as a hand mill
    you could see if you looked closely that the top ring
that turned in the other had been carved long before in the form
    of a fox lying nose in tail seeming to be
asleep the features worn almost away where it
    had gone around and around grinding grain and salt
to go into the dark and to go on and remember

This first section of the poem is essentially a description of some things the speaker and his friend see on a trip in the mountains: particularly an old mill, outside which the objects that used to be inside it are now "arranged . . . to wait pale in the daylight out on the open mountain / after whatever they had been made for was over." That is, they are now antiques, for sale. The grammatical structure and thought movement are, because of the lack of punctuation, fundamentally paratactic: that is, the grammatical structure puts on the same plane thoughts and events that in ordinary writing are usually organized hierarchically, and thus creates unexpected (but also very real) connections. As in so much contemporary poetry, therefore, the thinking is by its very nature associative, moving from one to another related, but not necessarily predictable, idea.

The poem is quick, leaping, intuitive. These qualities are, however, counterbalanced by the anecdotal and narrative: "On a road through the mountains with a friend many years ago / I came to a curve on a slope. . . ." This narrative grounding situates the poem firmly, which then allows the poet to step out at will and make associations and observations and digressions that are often quite strange, but always believable.

It is precisely this generous willingness to establish a narrative framework that allows the poet very quickly to move into a deeper state of perception: "I came to a curve on a slope where a clear stream / flowed down flashing across dark rocks through its own / echoes that could neither be caught nor forgotten." This movement, so natural and strange, is characteristic not only of this poem but of Merwin's poetry throughout his career, and reminds me of Cézanne, who works in the areas where figuration starts to become abstraction, or Coltrane, who would, by grounding his composition in melody, be able to bring the listener along with him out into the far regions of chaos and noise and then return.

I often say to my students—and it is still so funny and strange to me to think that I am no longer a student but have them myself, because in my mind, especially in relation to poetry, I will always be one—that without clarity, it is not possible to have true mystery. By "clarity" I mean a sense in the reader that what is being said on the surface of the poem is not a scrim or a veil deliberately hiding some other hidden, inaccessible certainty. Clarity in poetry is for me a kind of generosity, a willingness to be together with the reader in the same place of uncertainty and striving for understanding. To give the impression that something important is happening, but that the mere reader cannot have access to it without some kind of special esoteric knowledge, strikes me as deeply ungenerous, even cruel.

Merwin's poems have always been mysterious, generous, and clear, knowing in their unknowingness. Often this effect is achieved through the telling of a simple story. In *The Vixen*, as in much of Merwin's poetry, the combination of narrative structure and associative/paratactic movement makes it possible for Merwin to do something else essential to the effect of these poems: to move quietly and confidently into an aphoristic, truth-telling mode that is somehow full of deep personal compassion but also disembodied. These aphoristic moments seem almost to emerge from the natural world as truths as undeniable as animals or weather.

Beneath their simple, generous surfaces, the poems are often very complex, especially in their treatment of time. "The Furrow" begins in contemplation and ends in aphorism, and therefore seemed at the time quite unfashionable, not only in its noble and unironic willingness to explore the psychology of the narrator but also in its overt thinking about the landscape as a metaphorical way to understand a human situation.

The Furrow

Did I think it would abide as it was forever
    all that time ago the turned earth in the old garden
where I stood in spring remembering spring in another place
    that had ceased to exist and the dug roots kept giving up
their black tokens their coins and bone buttons and shoe nails
    made by hands and bits of plates as the thin clouds
of that season slipped past gray branches on which the early
    white petals were catching their light and I thought I knew
something of age then my own age which had conveyed me
    to there and the ages of the trees and the walls and houses
from before my coming and the age of the new seeds as I
    set each one in the ground to begin to remember
what to become and the order in which to return
    and even the other age into which I was passing
all the time while I was thinking of something different

The "it" of the first line of the poem refers, most obviously, to the nearest antecedent, the furrow. The speaker is asking himself whether, when he first dug the furrow and planted the seeds, he thought that "it," this strip of dug-up earth, would always "abide as it was forever," that is, continue for all time to be the way it was. Of course part of him did not, since he was planting seeds, which he presumably thought (or at least hoped) would grow. But part of him probably did assume or think (even though his conscious mind would have been aware in a logical sense that this was not the case) that the earth would always stay this way, dug up, disrupted, in a state of change.

In addition to the basic meaning of the first line, and beyond this particular situation of gardening, obviously this question has a larger, more allegorical context. "It" seems to be not merely the furrow but also an unspecified feeling: maybe a state of being or a time in life. It's hard to say right away at the beginning of the poem. The peculiar combination of specificity (the furrow) and multiple possibility (the unspoken huge feeling or idea to which the word "it" also points) is what gives the poem its immediate air of significance. *Furrow* is, literally, an agricultural term. But it is also, more familiarly for most of us, what a forehead does when one is confused or troubled. A reader can easily imagine the narrator, who in the third line is contemplating a previous stage in his life with a furrowed brow, trying (like the reader!) to think through something important, but also a bit elusive, right there in front of him.

This poem is characteristic of many in *The Vixen*. It begins with a clear, direct narrative situation. Someone is standing and looking at "the old garden" and thinking about how he planted seeds there. But the more I read the poem, the more I realize how complex it is, especially in its relationship to time. Merwin actually embeds at least four different periods in the poem. There is the current time, when the speaker is looking at the garden. There is the earlier spring, when the narrator made the furrow and planted the seeds. And there is the earlier spring than that one, the one the narrator is remembering he remembered as he planted: "I stood in spring remembering spring in another place / that had ceased to exist." And finally there is the much older time when these objects—"their black tokens their coins and bone buttons and shoe nails / made by hands and bits of plates"—first found their way into the earth the narrator is digging up.

So underneath this simple-seeming poem is actually quite a complex layering of time and memory. Now, in the current time, looking at the garden, the narrator remembers how he thought at the time when he was planting that he knew something important about life: "I thought I knew / something of age then my own age which had conveyed me / to there and the ages of the trees and the walls and houses / from before my coming and the age of the new seeds as I / set each one in the ground."

Maybe he did know something important then. But he knows something even more important now. At that time, even though all he could see was change and disruption and the hope and efforts to start something new, a new stage in his own life was already coming to be. The poem ends with a statement that both is particular to this narrator's life and experience and feels aphoristic: we are always passing into new stages, while all the time we are thinking of something different. In isolation this seems banal, but when this statement is reached at the end of the poem, it has the force of quiet revelation.

Paradoxically, wonderfully, when such statements seem to come out of nowhere—reached by associative methods and not by accretive logic—they feel all the more convincing. And this, I think, is one of the things we truly love about poetry, this ability to hear wisdom that feels truly wise yet also disembodied, as though it comes from the world itself.

At the end of another poem, "White Morning," the speaker and some other people go out to cut branches from trees in order to "cut handles that would last." The final lines of the poem cycle through many of the modes I have mentioned above, to chilling, enormous effect:

> the crows were calling around me to white air
> I could hear their wings dripping and hear small birds with lights
> breaking in their tongues the cold soaked through me I was able
> after that morning to believe stories that once
> would have been closed to me I saw a carriage go under
> the oaks there in full day and vanish I watched animals there
> I sat with friends in the shade they have all disappeared
> most of the stories have to do with vanishing

Everything is in those lines: the precision of natural description, the strange temporal destabilization of seeing this carriage, maybe from a different era, that appears and disappears, and the last two lines which quickly tell a little story, move paratactically into an observation, and then finish with anecdote.

Mostly though, reading them again and again, those last two lines of the poem fill me with sweet, contradictory feelings: agreement that "most of the stories" do in fact "have to do with vanishing," as well as sadness for the fact that so many of my beloved ones from the days when I was reading *The Vixen* have, like the "friends in the shade," also vanished to me now, and also joy in remembering the possibility of sudden awareness that reading and writing poems can at any time bring to me.

To Shine after It Has Gone

Resonance in W. S. Merwin's *The Vixen*

Jeanie Thompson

W. S. Merwin's lifelong contribution to American poetry began impressively when he was selected by W. H. Auden to receive the Yale Younger Poets prize in 1952. As has often been noted, during the 1950s and into the 1960s the Auden-tapped Yale Younger Poets, including Merwin, Adrienne Rich, and James Wright, radically changed their styles, moving into more open forms and leaving behind exclusively metrical verse or received forms to explore the "here and now" of poetry. The change is immediately apparent in the poems' lines: open-ended, scattered across the page, sometimes unpunctuated, and at first blush abandoning known signposts for the casual reader.

In an introductory lecture on Merwin's poetic trajectory, given at Spalding University in 2006, Thomas Byers called this new style "far less formal and ornate, with less highly conventionalized diction and a more openly lyric voice." Quoting Charles Altieri, Byers noted that Merwin and the Yale Younger Poets in his generation moved, in the 1960s and 1970s, "from symbolism (modernism) to immanence (the mode of the first wave of postmodern poetry)." The poems of this period don't "impose order on chaos, or rise out of the chaos of daily life into art's 'well wrought urn.'" Rather, "[t]he poet remains down in the field, finding or generating meaning in the process of ongoing encounter with the things and creatures and experiences that are found there."[1]

For the purpose of studying the evolution of Merwin's poetics, the question becomes, how does Merwin craft his lines in "the process of ongoing encounter" with what he finds in his field of poetry? For Merwin the field is personal and universal, immediate and historic. Students of poetic craft can understand better how Merwin's lines in *The Vixen*,[2] which was published more than forty years after the Yale Younger Poets prize launched his career, mark an apex of experimentation with the poetic line. The book is first and foremost about an ongoing encounter with "the things and creatures and experiences" in the region of southwest France where Merwin has long maintained a home. But the book also reflects Merwin's lifelong encounter with the complexities of human utterance as it is shaped in open form poetry.

Because the poems in *The Vixen* all employ the same type of alternately indented line, they have a somewhat uniform look on the page. The line shifts through various patterns of syntactical combination, caesura and enjambment, repetition, and stress patterns, always moving forward with an energy derived from the alternating indentation of the left margin, balanced by the return of the line itself, and played out through a variety of line endings. In a review of *The Vixen* in 1996, Richard Howard called these lines "loose Alexandrines" of twelve to fifteen syllables.[3]

When one first enters the poems of *The Vixen*, there is the jolt of apparently run-on thoughts that on closer examination prove to be unpunctuated sentences or statements. And yet the poems often move as narratives, stories the speaker tells of returning to a place from his past. In "Fox Sleep," traveling a back road so remote it seems like dream, the speaker encounters antique objects arranged like icons:

> in a handful of sunlight that made the slates on the silent
> mill by the stream glisten white above their ruin
> and a few relics of the life before had been arranged
> in front of the open mill house to wait
> pale in the daylight out on the open mountains
> after whatever they had been made for was over
> the dew was drying on them and there were few who took that road
> who might buy one of them and take it away somewhere
> to be unusual to be the only one
> to become unknown a wooden bed stood there on rocks

In the last two lines, three succeeding infinitives slow the poem, which then comes to a rather abrupt halt with the image of a bed set on rocks. Here the speaker finds the emblem of the vixen carved in stone, almost faded, almost gone. The chance finding of this image in a remote locale underscores the need to be attentive:

> and among them a ring of white stone the size of an
> embrace set into another of the same size
>
> . . . .
>
> you could see if you looked closely that the top ring
> that turned in the other had been carved long before in the form
> of a fox lying nose in tail seeming to be
> asleep the features worn almost away . . .

In the book's narrative, a totem animal, the vixen, becomes identified with something elusive and emblematic within the poet himself, culminating in the symphonic crescendo of "Vixen," the book's penultimate poem. The overall movement of the book, from the opening poem "Fox Sleep" to the closing poem "Given Day," is conditioned by the construction of the line itself. The line is organic, taking shape in patterns that evoke the passage of time, memory, self-revelation, confession, and ecstatic union. Key to all of these is the notion of *resonance*—that an image continues to live after we have heard it or seen it initially, that a line resonates in the way that a struck bell sounds, in waves that move out from the original object into time and our imaginations, and that our lives continue in our own memories as reconstructed and relived moments. Of course, a line of poetry resonates for us each time we reread it, and the construction of Merwin's lines teaches us how to be still and listen. Just as the vixen is mercurial, appearing frozen in time as a stone carving in "Fox Sleep" or streaking like light through "places in the silence after the animals" in "Vixen," so Merwin's lines organically accommodate what is necessary.

"Fox Sleep" is a five-part, first-person narrative poem, moving through time much as the individual lines do—entering the scene and then qualifying it, referring to memory and actual objects, commenting on the speaker's role in the past and present of the landscape. There is a sense of cinematic montage, as if the credits were rolling over these lines. The sections of this poem are edited together much like a film, and the point where one section ends prepares our eye for where to look in the next section.

Academy Award–winning film editor Walter Murch and novelist and poet Michael Ondaatje, who have collaborated on adaptations of literature in film, discuss the fascinating parallel between poetic lines and film editing in *The Conversations*. Murch says that the film editing process can teach us a lot about how poetic lines are "cut together."[4] Merwin's lines are cut together without punctuation here, as they have been since he famously dropped punctuation from his poems in the early 1960s. Like his earlier poems, the poems in *The Vixen* instruct us how to read them. But because of the bond the line pattern creates with the content to generate an energized motion of poetic thought, feel more tightly knit than the poems of *The Lice* (1967) or *The Carrier of Ladders* (1970).

In his contribution to the W. S. Merwin tribute issue of *Many Mountains Moving*, originally published in 2001 and included in this volume, Forrest Gander considers the poem "Substance" from *The Vixen*. Gander observes that "the poem's very form becomes an expression of both continuity and change. . . . As though to indicate the backward and forward motion of the poem's time, the line steps in front and returns repeatedly to the left margin. . . . the poem's syntax and punctuation . . . all intensify the [poem's] theme." For Gander and other poets who have assiduously studied the craft and content of Merwin's poems, there is the promise of unity of form and intention toward an awareness of our place in the construct of time.

In an interview that Jonathan Weinert and I conducted at Spalding University in 2006, also included in this collection, Merwin stated that "the line is a form" and if a poem works, "it *is* its form." This is the basic manifesto of early modern poetry and later "open form poetry" as it has evolved since Pound dashed off the two-line poem "In a Station of the Metro." Merwin takes the idea further by asserting, "What makes something a line has been shifting since one began to try to write things down." The line, Merwin says,

> is not bearing any part of the meaning obviously in itself. It looks to be purely formal, and yet there's no such thing happening there. So that's what I mean by "innocent of any / signal." And yet all forms empower what they're the form *of*; they make it possible. If you take a sonnet of

Shakespeare and write it out in prose, you begin to puzzle your head about all sorts of things that weren't puzzling before, because the form makes them clear. The form *is* an empowerment.

Merwin agrees that the poems in *The Vixen* are composed of lines that work like a "kind of enjambed statement," as Richard Howard described them in his review of *The Vixen* in *Boston Review*. For Howard, Merwin's virtuoso sentences "no longer break off, or down, or even up as they used to do in his books of ecstatic impoverishment. Now the punctuated lines of 12 to 15 syllables make use, rather, of enjambment as their only marker, the rest, or rather the restlessness being left to an unbroken voice patiently weaving its account of presence."[5]

Merwin's and Howard's comments provide a key to understanding the elasticity of the lines in *The Vixen*. These lines move with an urgency of telling; they push for meaning, become self-revelatory, and set up an expectation of form while not exactly fulfilling it. The very shape of the line—how it holds the syntax that moves across it—is the molecular structure of the poem. And remembering Murch's observation that lines are cut together like scenes of film, we can begin to understand how to read Merwin's lines.

Approaching the poems of *The Vixen* on the page, one sees them as *shapes* before entering the words, as one always does with poetry. Each poem seems built like a masonry wall: they appear solid from a distance, but upon approach one can see the brick laid in an interlocking pattern. Merwin's sentences run together without punctuation, yet most are complete clauses with subject and verb, or piled-up dependent or subordinate clauses waiting for the main clause to come along. Because the poems are all written in the same style, the same created form, we learn to trust the technique as it becomes familiar to us. Once we trust, we are open, and the poems begin to occur to us in the way that Merwin suggests that images occur to poets, not by any "act of will" or contrivance.[6] The poems are authentic, trustworthy, *resonant*—their meanings extend beyond their endings, continuing to sound after the initial act of reading the poem is complete.

The resonant line in *The Vixen* often balances an element of time, either apprehending its passage or experiencing it outright. Howard notes that the poems in *The Vixen* generally follow a three-part pattern to tell stories of people, objects, and the passage of time. Indeed, this collection can be read as a sequence, and the resonant line is key to the "temporal structure" Howard posits when he suggests that Merwin's book of "64 linked poems" is similar to Tennyson's *In Memoriam* and is thus a sequence.[7]

The Vixen, Howard proposes, employs "a repeating formula," which bolsters the sequence theory, as most poetic sequences employ repeating structures of various kinds:

> . . . not a recurrent rhyme scheme but a temporal structure almost as insistent as the great Victorian's. . . . There will be an opening phrase such as "once," or "at the beginning," or "this was the day when," or "in the long evening of April"—sometimes extended to constitute an opening line, as "one dark afternoon in the middle of the century." . . . Then comes the argument, in the operatic sense of that word, a sort of struggle the poet has with himself to endure whatever loss or loosening he has to report. . . . And then the sign-off, the removal of his consciousness from the circumstance which is perceived to be one that will continue without him . . .[8]

"In the Doorway," which appears about midway in the collection, is typical of this repeating formula and balances delicately on lines that move with a series of inversions and mirror effects, beginning with the setting in the title and on to the tactile particularity of the door itself:

> From the stones of the door frame cold to the palm
>   that breath of the dark sometimes from the chiselled
> surfaces and at others from the places between them
>   that chill and air without season that acrid haunting
> that skunk ghost welcoming without welcome faithful without
>   promise echo without echo . . .

These lines set the poem's tone and achieve what Howard calls the prelude. Developing the argument, the poem moves in a much more fluid way, and the ending is laced with a wealth of sensory elements that evoke emotion. Smells embody what eludes him like scent trails he picks up and loses, the scent of *abiding, finding again, touching, not being there*, among others that pungently haunt him:

> that smell of abiding
> and not staying of a night breeze remembered only

> in passing of fox shadow moss in autumn the bitter
> ivy the smell of the knife blade and of finding again
> knowing no more but listening the smell of touching and going
> of what is gone the smell of touching and not being there

Dependent on paradox, "In the Doorway" is itself a point of entry and leaving—a liminal space. Merwin's nod to Heraclitus, which pervades *The Vixen*, crystallizes here in a sixteen-line poem: time is constant flux, and only our attempt to shape it in acts such as poetry renders it comprehensible.

One of the strongest examples of Howard's formula is "Snake," which presents a seven-line statement, or preamble, prior to the opening phrase. The preamble is not actually a full sentence but is two dependent clauses, each begining with a temporal anaphora, "when it seemed . . . ," the first clause spanning four lines and the second spanning two:

> When it seemed to me that whatever was holding
> me there pretending to let me go but then bringing
> me back each time as though I had never been gone
> and knowing me knowing me unseen among those rocks
> when it seemed to me that whatever that might be
> had not changed for all my absence and still was not changing

After a suspenseful buildup, the main clause finally begins on line 7, though it also has two temporal qualifiers. This is what Howard calls the opening phrase: "once in the middle of the day late in that time / I stood up from the writings unfinished on the table. . . ." And of course the opening phrase leads us to the argument—something unfinished, or something stopped in process, the struggle. The poem continues:

> in the echoless stone room looking over the valley
> I opened the door and on the stone doorsill
> where every so often through the years I had come
> upon a snake lying out in the sunlight I found
> the empty skin like smoke on the stone with the day
> still moving in it and when I touched it and lifted
> all of it the whole thing seemed lighter than a single
> breath . . .

It is worth pausing to note how the simile "the empty skin like smoke on the stone" combines a concrete image, the empty snakeskin, with something ethereal at best, the smoke on the stone. But how can smoke, which is moving, reside on stone, which is static? At this point, the line resonates at such a pitch that we must stop, but the simile is truly charged alive with the time reference: "with the day still moving in it." So the smoke is actually the visual embodiment of the day itself, the passage of time. The fluidity of the enjambed lines makes this possible. We are slowed to such a point that we can be open to this highly textured image. Is it simile, is it metaphor, or some combination of the two?

Following Howard's mapping, there is a "removal of consciousness" at the end of the poem—a physical removal of the snake's consciousness with its shed skin and with the human's apprehension of the moment.

> and then I was gone and that time had changed and when
> I came again many years had passed and I saw
> one day along the doorsill outside that same room
> a green snake lying out in the sunlight watching me

With the deftness of these enjambed sentences and lines that alternately indent, Merwin is able to achieve an agility of image, concocting the magical: "I found / the empty skin like smoke on the stone with the day / still moving in it." The snake, a real *particular* thing, has distracted the poet from his real, *particular* task of creating a poem. But the snake has shed its skin, leaving even the color of its eyes behind, and who is to say that the poet's work is any less real than this skin? Is the poet's work the shed skin of his momentary apprehension of the image? We are given an analogue here: the poet interrupted is somehow analogous to the snake in the doorway, sunning, shedding, and leaving his colors, an exemplar of time's progress/process. The lines shed themselves from sentence to sentence as well. This is one of Merwin's recurring themes in *The Vixen* and other works: that nature provides an analogue for humanity, even if humans rarely pause to decode and make sense of it.

The syntax of "The Snake" coils for nearly seven lines before the actual story begins, but once it does, the lines remain mostly regular until the line "breath and then I was gone and that time had changed and when . . ." is allowed to uncoil and lengthen out with no fewer than four conjunctions, as if the line is literally stretching. The poem slows slightly here and prepares us for the next big temporal leap, which is handled with two short enjambed statements, "I came again many years had passed," and the poet sees the same snake (or so he thinks) lying in the same sunlight. The poem ends with the stunning statement that, like the opening coiled lines, coils upon itself, slowing us down to apprehend it: "even from the eyes the skin loosens leaving the colors / that have passed through it and the colors shine after it has gone."

Upon reading this, someone may simultaneously admire the metaphor of the shedding of memory and also ask, "Is this biologically correct?" The answer may be no, but the hypnotically coiled image and Howard's "withdrawal of consciousness" combine to keep us wondering. Like an architectural underpinning, the form of the line makes this complicated syntactical structure and resulting statements possible. The coiled energy of this poem derives from the spring of that line: the steady left margin indents every other line, the surprising right margin ends at key points in the syntax. The game of reading only the last words of the lines is instructive here, forming a précis for the poem itself: *holding, bringing, gone, rocks, be, changing, time, table, valley, doorsill, come, found, day, lifted, single, when, saw, room, me, colors, gone*. Strong verbs, the punch of single-syllable nouns, and time elements anchor the poem.

The collection's not-quite-title poem, "Vixen," embodies the vision first sensed in "Fox Sleep," the opening overture. Merwin has admonished readers in several interviews and in remarks before readings not to take this animal as symbol but rather to see the vixen literally. In the Spalding University interview he notes that the image of the animal, the vixen, "is more complicated than a symbol. The vixen is an appearing and disappearing presence that is there all the time." He affirms that the vixen is "something that has come to you and left you and comes back to you" and that it exemplifies the "wildness" Thoreau identified: "It's the most precious thing we have. And everybody has it."

Pressing on, I asked, "Does that somehow play in with the energy of the lines, these statements? Is that where the energy's coming from?" He said, "Well, I hope so," and proceeded to talk a little more about the prosody of verse as an "expectation that is set up but is never quite fulfilled."

Whatever the nature of the vixen in Merwin's poetic mythology, the reso-
nant line is the structure *upon which* or *by which* or *through which* the vision
occurs to the poet—not an act of will but a moment of being open to the
occurrence of the image. The engine of the resonant lines working together
with regularity (the alternating left margin) but also with possibility (the
variety of line endings) opens his poetic consciousness, as they circle back
to the totem of truth that streaks through the book just as the vixen, "the
comet of stillness, the princess of what is over," appears, disappears, and
reappears throughout the book.

"Vixen" is the penultimate poem in the book, following "Distant
Morning," a poem of the compression of time and space: "We were a time of
our own." The poem prepares us for the moment of the vixen's appearance
on the next page. Turn the page following "Vixen" and the book closes
with "Given Day," once again a moment that asks us to pause and remember
how "When I wake, I find. . . ." A ringing line of clarity appears almost
dead-center in the poem: "then one at a time I remember without under-
standing. . . ." Preparation for the moment of apprehension in Merwin's
poetic vision requires holding consciousness lightly. One remembers in an
instant, as if given a gift.

In "Vixen," a poem of such urgent direct address that he cannot settle
on how to name her, Merwin acquiesces by cataloging her facets. She is
a comet, a princess, a high note, an aura, a keeper of secrets, a warden, a
sibyl, a window; she is patient. Merwin invites us through the seamless
resonant lines of this poem to see her with him:

> Comet of stillness princess of what is over
> high note held without trembling without voice without sound
> aura of complete darkness keeper of the kept secrets
> of the destroyed stories the escaped dreams the sentences
> never caught in words warden of where the river went
> touch of its surface sibyl of the extinguished
> window onto the hidden place and the other time

The address gives over to the description of the setting, making way for the
poet's most direct address to the vision that presents herself to him:

> at the foot of the wall by the road patient without waiting
> in the full moonlight of autumn at the hour when I was born
> you no longer go out like a flame at the sight of me

Beginning the line with "you" emphasizes the culmination of the address with a short hard stress, and there is a clear full stop in the poem's movement right after "at the sight of me," as if there were end-stopped punctuation. The poet has invoked the vixen, naming and renaming her, and has built up to the moment in which he can most directly say to her that he *believes in her* because she does not "go out like a flame at the sight of me." His metaphor of fire not extinguished conjures images of ritual, creativity, love, and life. This long address to the vixen travels across ten full lines and ends with the word *me*. Just as the lines are anchoring and opening for Merwin, the address to this totem animal allows him to come back home and reach a level of self-knowledge and peace. The most important stressed words are first "you" and then "me," which underscore a sense of continually seeking union.

We see her as he has seen her, as he believes in her. And we can acknowledge how apprehension of this image from the visible world makes the poet whole. This is an incredibly intimate moment because it contains a reverence usually afforded a beloved, or a deity, and it also reveals something Merwin clearly has felt slip through his poet fingers before ("on the breathless night / on the bridge with one end"). Much can be made of how these familiar dreamscape images of anxiety, breathlessness, and a bridge with only one end overlap with Merwin's consciousness of the precarious ecology of our planet and his dedication to conservation. In this poem as perhaps no other, we experience the vixen as he does, as totem for his poetry and his humanity. We readers, fellow poets, fellow humans, are invited to also claim kin with Merwin's vixen:

> you are still warmer than the moonlight gleaming on you
> even now you are unharmed even now perfect
> as you have always been now when your light paws are running
> on the breathless night on the bridge with one end I remember you
> when I have heard you the soles of my feet have made answer

As Howard has shown us, there is a withdrawal of consciousness as these poems end. One cannot remain in an ecstatic vision, because the very nature of it is mercurial—it is *a-static*. One may abide in it in memory, in poetry. Thus as Merwin continues to address the vixen, his tone changes to one of greater detachment, employing diction of impermanence such as *waked, slipped, difference, contradictions, crumbling*, and the phrase *as long as it lasted*.

> when I have seen you I have waked and slipped from the calendars
> from the creeds of difference and the contradictions
>   that were my life and all the crumbling fabrications
> as long as it lasted . . .

At this point in the poem, the lines begin to tighten; they contain fewer short phrases strung together as signals of the apprehending moment for the poet and are more of a piece of line/syntax, indicating his synthesis of the experience into statement, "until something that we were / had ended when you are no longer anything / let me catch sight of you again going over the wall." The human consciousness that has so intimately communed with the vixen somewhat dissipates into a greater human statement: "and before the garden is extinct and the woods are figures / guttering on a screen let my words find their own / places in the silence after the animals." So we are left to consider the last lines in a broader human context. While Merwin is always and utterly personal, he is also universal. He closes "Vixen" with an extinct garden that could be the earth; "woods" guttering on a screen, which suggest humanity's extinction on a barren planet; and the poignant human desire to speak to one another *in poetry* after this vision. A poem that begins in an intensively private and ecstatic moment leaves us with a kind of lesson, an admonishment to do our work, not just as poets but as tenders of the garden to which we have been granted entry, and also to be prepared for the consequences of failure. This is a lot to comprehend, analyze, and act upon. Only through its compression into poetic lines is such an experience transferable to others. A resonant line built of regular form *and* openness makes it possible.

The Vixen exemplifies the bond between an elastic, resonant line and the poet's experience of the passage of time, charged with deepening human understanding in a historically and personally resonant place perhaps more acutely than any of Merwin's previous collections. Representing a turning point in the development of Merwin's line, the poems in *The Vixen* are tempered by lyricism, narrative, personal confession, longing, fondness, and release. Merwin himself cited the book as a breakthrough moment that signaled how he might write the longer work *The Folding Cliffs* (1998): that is, the collection led him to a sustaining form.[9] In *The Vixen*, the lines migrate to a new locale that provides the necessary sustenance for survival, resonating across the years of Merwin's work, moving him forward to new awareness and an increasingly pure bond of form and content: a line that moves, resonating with energy and variety to hold the complex of his poetic life—and ours.

Prolegomena to Any Future Reading of The Folding Cliffs

H. L. Hix

In what follows I present not a reading of W. S. Merwin's long narrative poem *The Folding Cliffs* (1998) but a sequence of linked meditations reflecting—in a way I think the poem invites—on the conditions for a sound reading. To put this another way, this essay attempts to *point toward* and *prepare for*, rather than to *be*, a reading of the poem.

To Get It or Not to Get It

Hamlet's Claudius "got it."

During the performance Hamlet commissions the players to give for the court, just after Lucianus pours poison in Gonzago's ear, Claudius rises and stops the play, commanding, "Give me some light. Away!" (3.2.269).[1] In an alternative *Hamlet*, Claudius might have let the play continue, at its end explaining to Ophelia certain of its subtle biblical allusions, and later discussing with Gertrude in their bedchamber clues to the psychological motivations of the characters, all lucidly and with clear conscience. But his explicating the play in this way, even doing so with the utmost accuracy, would only demonstrate that he had missed the point altogether. In the actual *Hamlet* we don't know whether Claudius could have summarized the plot or identified instances of foreshadowing. His interrupting the play, though, shows that he got it.

His getting it, in other words, is not contingent on his "understanding" the play in the way we normally mean that term, as an ability to explain the play to others, identify literary devices at work in the play, account for details of the work, and so on. Claudius might have a very full understanding in that sense and still not get it at all. His getting it *is* contingent on his recognizing that whatever else it may also be about, the play is about *him*. If he sees himself in the play, rightly ascertaining that Lucianus is he and he is Lucianus, and that he and Lucianus are in the wrong, he gets it; if not, not.

There are differences between the two cases (e.g., the play has been manipulated by Hamlet to be about Claudius *in particular*, about him in a way that it is not about other audience members), but I want to assert a similarity between Claudius's viewing of the play and a contemporary reader's reading of W. S. Merwin's *The Folding Cliffs*. A reader of *The Folding Cliffs*, I contend, will "get it" if and only if he or she correctly recognizes himself or herself in the poem and arrives through that recognition at a clearer self-understanding.

Two Questions about a Work

Emphasis in the early reception of a literary work typically falls heavily on the question "Is it good?" It is easy to see why: reviews, for instance, function as gatekeepers, steering readers toward certain works and away from others. But its being *motivated* doesn't make heavy emphasis on the question "Is it good?" *ideal*. "Is it good?," asked as the primary question, the question that orients one's engagement with the poem, enervates the poem and trivializes the encounter with it. It suppresses the more crucial question "What is at stake?" and settles in advance the reader's role and task.

Taking "Is it good?" as the primary question treats the poem as possessed of a (singular, settled) value, which I am to discern. I assume the role of judge and the task of subjecting to order the otherwise chaotic. I hold the poem up to a preset standard and determine whether or not it matches. In an increasingly "global" society in which the privileged experience pluralism as a danger that culminates in terror and war, "Is it good?" is a tempting approach to the poem, because it settles the matter of inclusion in, or exclusion from, consideration. The ultimate fulfillment of the question "Is it good?" is canon-fixing, in which the status quo is secured by acknowledging and affirming what satisfies existing standards and dismissing what does not.

"What is at stake?" does not settle in advance either my role or my task, but includes them within the question. "Is it good?" places me above the poem, makes it subject to my determination; "What is at stake?" sets me face to face with the poem, makes me just as subject to its determination as it is to mine. "Is it good?" is an aesthetic question; "What is at stake?" is an existential question. "Is it good?" is inherently monological and impositional, in contrast to the inherently dialogical and reciprocal "What is at stake?" "Is it good?" is a relatively closed and confining question, "What is at stake?" a relatively open and expansive question.

Making "Is it good?" the primary question puts the cart before the horse and contributes to the liminality of poetry in our culture. A reliance on authority (she won the Pulitzer for her last book) rather than a willingness to judge for myself will be a likely result of asking "Is it good?" before asking "What is at stake?"

Two Examples of Not Getting It

Early critical judgments of the worth of *The Folding Cliffs*—early answers to the question "Is it good?"—diverged wildly. At one extreme, Michael Thurston offered lavish praise, saying that *The Folding Cliffs* "succeeds with power and grace."[2] Adam Kirsch staked out the other extreme, rebuking Merwin sternly for reducing an "inherently powerful story" to mere tendentiousness by "flattening truth into myth."[3]

Thurston's argument makes several points. First, he notes that *The Folding Cliffs* fills the last void in Merwin's otherwise complete and replete body of work. Merwin has written, he says, "in an astonishing variety of forms," including metrical verse and poetry in open forms, "prose memoirs and fiction, numerous translations, and even a verse drama."[4] Until *The Folding Cliffs*, though, the long narrative poem, which, Thurston notes parenthetically, has been, "in recent years, something of a prerequisite for the Nobel Prize," has "been missing from [Merwin's] oeuvre." Second, *The Folding Cliffs*, Thurston observes, "enables Merwin to treat at length" a thematic concern that "has recurred throughout Merwin's career," namely "the pain and damage of separation and division," a theme manifest with particular clarity in his poems by those titles: "Separation," from *The Moving Target* (1963), and "Division," from *Writings to an Unfinished Accompaniment* (1973).[5]

Thurston's third point heightens the praise. *The Folding Cliffs*, Thurston suggests, "is nothing less than the inauguration of a new poetic form, a form created through Merwin's reimagining of epic and narrative poetics." The reimagining is rooted in fulfillment of epic conventions: a beginning *in medias res*, inclusion of "embedded stories and genealogies," employment of "heightened diction," and development through "the slow accumulation of landmarks and recognizable relationships."[6] But the theme of separation and division contrasts it to traditional epic: "by situating Pi'ilani's life against the backdrop of Hawai'i's history," Thurston says, Merwin creates an "epic narrative of national dissolution,"[7] a work that is epic in scale but not in theme. In Thurston's terms, *The Folding Cliffs* becomes "a sort of anti-*Aeneid* for Hawai'i, an epic that treats not the founding of a city but the conquering, division, and dispersal of a people and its culture."[8]

Kirsch's evaluation of *The Folding Cliffs* occurs as half of a review that also examines Merwin's collection *The River Sound* (1999). Just as for Thurston *The Folding Cliffs* is representative, a culmination of Merwin's concerns, so for Kirsch *The Folding Cliffs* and *The River Sound* are representative, but rather than representing what is *good* about Merwin's work, they represent what is *bad*. The two books together "furnish," Kirsch says, "a full look at Merwin's style and sensibility, his interests and the problems that they entail."[9] Kirsch notes that Merwin explicitly avoids identifying *The Folding Cliffs* with either "the classical genre, the epic," or "the modern genre, the novel," preferring instead the more "neutral" status of "narrative," which commits itself only to the telling of a story without a concomitant commitment to *how* it will be told. The facts of the purportedly true story "comprise a strong and affecting tale," Kirsch says, that "could have been invented specifically to appeal to our cultural moment," because it would be "an ideal brief in the case against American colonialism."[10] The poem's being so ideal a brief means that one cannot read it without "a renewed awareness of the brutality and the arrogance that were certified with the seal of 'manifest destiny.'"[11]

Its occasioning of such renewed awareness Kirsch calls a "lesson" that is part of "Merwin's didactic intention," but Kirsch excludes the lesson from the poem: it "has nothing to do with poetry, or indeed with literature. It is political, or historical, or humanitarian," but not poetic. The only pertinent issues, on Kirsch's view, are those "raised by its two aesthetic ambitions, the poetic and the novelistic."[12] He does not explain how the poem maintains novelistic ambition in the face of its having ("appropriately," Kirsch opines) been denied to be a novel.[13]

The Judge Judged

Given two such radically opposed assessments of the poem as those of Thurston and Kirsch, one might shrug and sigh that there's no accounting for tastes. You say *tomayto,* I say *tomahto.* But there's another possibility: that we *are* accountable for our tastes, and that the stakes in a work of art such as a poem—such as *this* poem—include that accountability. It may be, in other words, that judgment is *reciprocal*: in judging I am judged. The being judged—the reciprocity of judgment—occurs whether or not it is recognized, and whether or not it is acknowledged, by the person judging.

Consider as an analogy observations made by Louis Mackey about medieval proofs of God's existence. Proofs of God's existence present themselves, like judgments of poems, as accurate statements about an external reality. But Mackey points out that "not all who prove the existence of God are proving the same thing," and "not everyone who proves the existence of God is proving it in the same way"; from which follows the observation that whether or not such proofs tell us anything about God, "the particular proof by which a philosopher chooses to demonstrate the existence of God tells us a great deal about his theological orientation and his philosophical disposition."[14] Mackey's point is that, as there is in physics no absolute space to award objectivity to assessments of movement, so there is in philosophy no absolute indifference to award objectivity to assessments of truth. "Though they may claim to have no beliefs not validated by logic and the evidence, all philosophers are guided in their thinking by prior commitments, religious or irreligious, as much as they are by reason"; all, Mackey alleges, "are trying to understand the world they *believe* they live in."[15]

Similarly, each of the two example judgments of Merwin's poem tells us about the critical orientation and poetic disposition of the judge. Thurston's evaluation reveals his sense that a poem's success results from its achieving a satisfying concord between generic conventions and thematic concerns. "The story," Thurston says, "provides Merwin with a driving narrative and attractive characters" at the same time that it enables him to "treat at length" his recurring theme of division/separation.[16]

Kirsch's evaluation reveals that for him poetry is a strictly aesthetic phenomenon isolated from other human realms such as politics and history. The two precedents Kirsch names as having created successful long narrative poems on the basis of style alone are Wordsworth and Milton, either of whom surely would be surprised to see his poetry treated as a proof text for the exclusion of political, historical, and humanitarian concerns. Wordsworth, after all, claims of his *Lyrical Ballads* that "if the views with which they were composed were indeed realised," the poems will "interest mankind permanently" because of the quality and multiplicity of their "moral relations."[17] In describing his plans for a poem to be called *The Recluse*, occasioned by *The Prelude* and with *The Excursion* as one of its parts, Wordsworth speaks of his "determination to compose a philosophical poem, containing views of Man, Nature, and Society."[18] Milton, for his part, opens the first book of *Paradise Lost* with an invocation to the "Heav'nly Muse" to illumine the darkness in him, "That to the highth of this great Argument / I may assert Eternal Providence, / And justify the ways of God to men."[19] Kirsch's desire to restrict poetry to style is flatly contradicted by his two exemplars: Wordsworth and Milton both, quite explicitly, claim for themselves and their poems "didactic intention," and claim such intention as an aspect of, not as something opposed to, the poems. For Wordsworth and Milton both, poetry is (and, if I read them correctly, *must be*) precisely what Kirsch says poetry isn't: political, historical, humanitarian, didactic.

Not all who ask whether a poem is good are asking the same thing. Thurston is asking about the adequacy of the poem to its own standards. "Is it good?" means to him something like "Does it employ conventions of genre in ways that aptly embody its themes?" Kirsch is asking about the adequacy of the poem to *his* standards. "Is it good?" means to him something like "Does it realize stylistic conventions I appreciate?" That Thurston and Kirsch apply different standards to the poem draws attention to the fact that the appropriate standard is not given but chosen; it is itself open to question. If we draw again on Mackey, we note that the choice of standard is a commitment intended to advance understanding of the world Thurston (or Kirsch) believes he lives in. That is, the reader, like the standard, is involved in, rather than hovering outside of or above, the negotiation in reading the poem.

More Questions Than One

If "Is it good?" represents more than one question, if judgment is reciprocal, if standards and the reader are in play just as the poem is, then it appears that in addition to "Is it good?" we might do well to ask such other questions as "What good does it invite from me?" (as John F. Kennedy in his inaugural address invited Americans to "ask not what your country can do for you—ask what you can do for your country"). To what best aspect of me does it appeal? To what form of plenitude am I invited by the poem? Opening the standard question in this way draws attention to the complexity of the interaction between poem and reader. I suggest that there are at least six elements of such interaction, so that the complexity of the poem-reader interaction can be insinuated by the following table.

	a. Poem	*b. Standards*	*c. Reader*
1. Poem's Standards	*1a. Does the poem fullfil its own standards?*	*1b. What are the poem's standards? Are they worthy?*	*1c. Do I fulfill the poem's standards?*
2. My Standards	*2a. Does the poem fullfill my standards?*	*2b. What are my standards? Are they worthy?*	*2c. Do I fulfill my own standards?*

The point of the chart is not to be exhaustive, only to make explicit the analogy with Mackey's observation by noting various questions a reader might be attempting to answer when she or he reads a poem. Thurston, I contend, asks 1a, whether the poem fulfills its own standards, and Kirsch asks 2a, whether the poem fulfills his (Kirsch's) standards. My assertion is that neither question, by itself, is enough. To be robust, my reading must ask all six questions, none of which is independent of or wholly separable from the others.

Thurston and Kirsch use their versions of "Is it good?" to foreclose other questions. So, for example, what Kirsch means by calling *The Folding Cliffs* didactic (and taking didacticism as inherently bad and antipoetic) is that, in answer to 2a, he finds the poem so far from fulfilling his standards that he refuses to entertain 1c as a live question. What he means by excluding historical or political content from poems is that any of the questions in row 1 are irrelevant, since his standards are the only ones that apply. If the poem's standards match my standards, then the questions in row 1 are superfluous, and if they do not match my standards, well, they ought to.

I suggest, though, that if the poem does fulfill its own standards but does not fulfill my standards, then a judicious spectator would ask what grounds there are for preferring one set of standards to the other, so the other questions on the chart would all be "live." My emphasis on the question "What is at stake?" can be formulated in terms of this chart. "Is it good?" asks either 1a or 2a reductively, in the sense that it tries to confine a reading to only one of the six questions. "What is at stake?," though, raises *all six* questions, sees them as inseparable from one another, and invites a dialogical rather than a monological reading. My claim about "getting it" is that a reading that does not ask more of the questions than one, and does not recognize them as interrelated with one another, and in particular does not pose 1c, is an empty reading, a reading that doesn't "get it."

The chart, in other words, suggests an ideal and a principle. The ideal is the convergence and harmony of answers to all the questions. Dissonance between answers to the questions ought to be minimized as far as possible. This is the means by which a poem may be didactic: if the poem does not fulfill my standards (2a) but does fulfill its own (1a), and if its standards by comparison prove more worthy (1b) than mine (2b), then I ought to change my standards in such a way that my fulfilling my own standards (2c) will entail fulfillment of the poem's standards (1c). The principle is to engage all six questions, rather than confining oneself as far as possible to one. In the relation between questions lies the poem's capacity for surprise. If my standards are taken for granted, the closure of the questions in row 1 is also a closure of my capacity for seeing anything other than my expectations. I am capable only of a reading that is a self-fulfilling prophecy.

An Example of Asking More Than One Question

In his response to Merwin's *The Folding Cliffs*, John Burt makes a valuable distinction between "verse which moves in the direction of conversation

and verse which moves in the direction of music."[20] The distinction aris-
es, Burt contends, because verse has a "dual allegiance . . . to talk and to
chant." He himself employs the distinction as a way to articulate just how
The Folding Cliffs does and does not fulfill its ambitions. He sees this dis-
tinction as "related but not identical to" the distinction between narrative
and lyric verse. Though narrative verse has been in decline, Burt notes that
narrative and lyric "remain continuously engaged with one another," since
lyric needs an implied narrative and narrative needs "moments of lyric
intensity."[21] But the distinction between narrative and lyric verse is not
enough for a reading of *The Folding Cliffs*, according to Burt, since though
The Folding Cliffs calls itself "A Narrative," it is *also*, he says, incantatory.
He calls Merwin "a great contemporary master of chant, and never more so
than when he seeks to set the foundation of his poem in the deepest stra-
tum he can imagine."[22]

Schematizing Burt's distinction, then:

	Talk	Chant
Model	Conversation	Music
Purpose	Manage unpredictability	Change consciousness
View of persons	Ordinary	Mythic
Condition of persons	Moral accountability	Possession
Portrayal of persons	Depicted	Invoked
Purported source	Author's intelligence	Voice speaking through author
Mode of reception	Heard and overheard	Heard only
Genre alliance	History	Epic
Period affinity	Modernity	Tradition

Burt calls incantation "a technology for inducing a change in conscious-
ness": to chant "is to work one's way into a special frame of mind sepa-
rate from one's usual state, and to listen to a chant is to align oneself with
that frame of mind."[23] Talk seeks to "render people in their ordinariness,"
with normal motivations and capacities, but chant "lends itself to mythic
character, to larger-than-life figures charged with *mana*, to characters
who are embodied forces";[24] as embodied forces, they are "possessed by
their acts and their feelings," in contrast to ordinary persons, who "make

decisions under conditions of partial ignorance, decisions for which they are to be morally called to account." Because characters in chant are mythic and possessed, incantation "seems not so much to depict them as to invoke them."[25]

Incantation seeks to be understood not as "the invention of its author's intelligence" but as "the incarnation of something which speaks through the author, something deep and inward but completely impersonal because deeper than personality, psychology, and biography."[26] Its embeddedness in the ordinary means that talk "is always both heard and overheard, and the overhearing is part of the variegation which is its life."[27] Chant closes the distance between hearing and overhearing: it "is never overheard in the way talk is overheard; one either gives oneself up to it or resists doing so." Chant tells mythic stories—"timeless stories, always inherited, never invented, older even than the characters whose acts they appear to record"[28]—so it allies itself with the epic, in contrast to talk, whose stories are timebound and political, and which therefore allies itself with history. Finally, chant is employed when a poem wishes "to align itself with tradition rather than modernity."[29]

Burt's approach contrasts with that of Thurston and Kirsch in that it raises all the questions, rather than raising one in a way that forecloses the others. For example, in this short passage all the questions are active:

> Sentence by sentence, Merwin can render talk. Line by line, he seems to wish to transform it into chant, and it resists him.
>
> The problem may have been inevitable given the poem's dual aims to tell the story of a relatively recent political conflict which occurred among basically modern people, and to root that story in eternity and myth. More or less contemporary political conflicts demand to be rendered in the style of talk. . . . But the versification of the poem as a whole has been chosen to align itself with tradition rather than modernity.[30]

"What are the poem's standards?" (1b) is the starting point: the poet strives for chant. But that raises 1a, "Does the poem fulfill its own standards?," to which Burt replies with the observation that the material resists chant. Burt's own standards (2b) become clear with his affirming as obvious that contemporary political matters insist on talk rather than chant. Those together imply an answer to 2a, that the poem is resisting Burt's standards. Also implied are responses to the questions in column c, "Do I fulfill the poem's standards?" and "Do I fulfill my own standards?" The poem's standards are depicted as admirable but unattainable, so I am left by default to fulfill my own rather than the poem's standards.

At Stake in *The Folding Cliffs*

Philosopher Alain Badiou stipulates a particular meaning of "truth," according to which a truth is "endowed with a transworldly and universal value,"[31] a "particular resistance" such that even though it occurs "in one world, it is valid *actually* for other worlds and *virtually* for all."[32] A truth is transtemporal, "produced with particular materials in a specific world," but "understood and usable in an entirely different world and across potentially vast spans of time."[33] Truths, Badiou says, can migrate. They have an "inviolate availability" that makes it "possible for them to be resuscitated and reactivated in worlds heterogeneous to those in which they were created" and gives them the power of "crossing over, as such, unknown oceans and obscure millennia."[34] Truths *apply*: "incorporating yourself within a truth's becoming consists in bringing to the body serving as the support of this truth everything within you that has an intensity comparable to what it is that allows you to identify with the primordial statement— *qua* the stigmata of the event in which the body has its source." Truth happens when "degree of identity . . . is maximal."[35] When Claudius sees that he is Lucianus, in other words.

What Badiou calls truth I would want to call likeness. If my love can be like a red, red rose, then is it possible for W. S. Merwin to be like Pi'ilani, and is it possible for me to be like Pi'ilani? Perhaps more accurately, can I *regard* myself as like Pi'ilani, or *make* myself like Pi'ilani? The most fundamental issue is not whether form and content relate properly (as Thurston affirms that they do) or whether purpose and genre relate properly (as Kirsch contends they do not), but whether my life and the poem relate properly. It is not self-evident that they *can* do so. The characters with whom we are invited to identify in *The Folding Cliffs*, including the protagonist, are Hawaiian, not European or American. The protagonist is female. W. S. Merwin is an American male, I am an American male, and everyone cited so far in this essay is a European or American male. As beneficiaries of wealth and security that were furthered by the Euro-American appropriation of Hawai'i, Merwin and I alike stand accused by the poem. That is, the poem's standards, according to which Europeans and Americans are the villains and Hawaiians the victims and the heroes of the poem, conflict with standards that, even if neither of us would nominally accept them, created living conditions that privilege Merwin and me both.

As a narrative whose protagonist resists the colonialism being imposed on her, *The Folding Cliffs* puts at stake the limits of one's engagement with the other. A reader of the poem—at least readers who are citizens of colonizing nations, but also, I suggest, *any* reader—faces an ethical and civic question that could be formulated in this way: *Can I contain/diminish my (material) encroachment on the other, and release/expand my (spiritual) identification with the other?* It is not self-evident that it is possible to do so meaningfully. Such works as Gayatri Spivak's "Can the Subaltern Speak?" and J. M. Coetzee's *Elizabeth Costello* convey something of how problematic the question is. I have no answer to the question: argumentation and other discourse may help me find my way to an answer but will not be themselves the answer. A reading of *The Folding Cliffs*, though, insofar as it poses, in relation to one another, all six questions in the chart discussed above, might impose this (vital) question on me, and might also aid me as I seek to address the question.

Raw Shore of Paradise

A Conversation with W. S. Merwin

Jeanie Thompson and Jonathan Weinert

—at Spalding University, Louisville, Kentucky, November 17, 2006

Jonathan Weinert: I want to start by asking you some questions about your latest collection, *Present Company*.[1] Your poems often make use of paradox to point to understandings that lie beyond what words can typically say. One of the central paradoxes in your work, I think, is the paradox or interplay between absence and presence. I think that this book, *Present Company*, turns in part on the paradox. I wonder if you could comment on that.

W. S. Merwin: I think paradox is built into language itself. We take the language wonderfully for granted once we start to be able to speak it, but every time we use a word, every time we use language, it's unique, and it's completely personal. Every word as we use it is completely our own, and yet it's not ours. We didn't invent it. It has a history that we don't know, which contains felt experience from many other lives and many other occasions, from every other time it's been used. So a word is in process of evolution all the time, and yet it's unique to that moment. That's one paradox.

The moment you have language, the moment you have expression of any kind, the word is not what it's expressing. It's always different, separate from it, and yet it's the most urgent and intimate way of dealing with it.

It both embodies what it's expressing and makes a distance from it. That's another paradox. The more present you try to make the moment, the more absent it becomes, although it becomes something that you can deal with. The present is something that you can't get closer to, and yet that's not what you're trying to do with speech—you're trying to embody the present and pass it on at the same time. That's the paradox, and it's always there.

JW: There's a sense in your work that the present is not exactly present, that it's always slipping away—that it's difficult or impossible to grasp.

WSM: Well, that too. When you're using language, you're using the past, you're not using the present. You don't invent language on the spot. If you did nobody could understand you. When you're trying to describe the present, and when you're trying to imagine the present, when you're trying to *think* of the present, you're actually thinking of the past. The reason we recognize each other is because of our entire lives, you know—we know what other people are, to some degree.

JW: One poem in *Present Company* is addressed directly to *absence*. I wonder if you could read that for us.

WSM: All of the poems in the book are in the second person, so they're all addressed to something, to somebody, or to some concept.

To Absence

Raw shore of paradise
which the long waves reach
just as they fail
one after the other
bare strand beyond which
at times I believe I see
as in a glass darkly
what I know here
and now cannot be
a face I can never touch
a gaze that cannot stay
which I catch sight of

still turned upon me
following me
from under the sky
of your groundless country
that has no syllable of its own
what good to you
are the treasures beyond
words or number
that you seize forever
unmapped imperium
when only here
in the present
which has lost them
only now
in the moment you
have not yet taken
does anyone know them
or how rare they are

JW: Thank you. I think something very interesting happens in this poem. At first, it isn't at all clear which world the "shore of paradise" that you mention in the poem belongs to. On closer reading, it's clear that absence itself is that shore. In what sense is absence the threshold of paradise?

WSM: Have you ever lost anything?

JW: Yes.

WSM: So you know. [laughter]

JW: So it's the world into which everything we lose disappears. . . . But it's stored up there somehow, as well.

WSM: Well, what's beyond the raw shore of paradise? Absence.

JW: But it's not a negation, it seems to me.

WSM: No. By that time, affirmation and negation—that's a polarity that doesn't mean anything.

JW: So it's like a treasure house in which everything is stored, yet somehow out of reach.

WSM: Yes. Our lives are made of it. Everything in your childhood is there, after all. What would your life be without what you remember from your childhood? You may have hated it, but it's terribly important to you.

JW: The poems in *Present Company* are all written in the form of odes, or apostrophes, and as such they bring to mind Pablo Neruda and Keats. I wonder if you had them in mind as you were writing this book.

WSM: Well, I didn't, and of course as I got into it I suddenly thought, "Ah, someone's going to be reminded of Neruda." I never thought of these poems as odes, but I guess that's what they are, and the odes that they're closest to are the Neruda odes, where he simply takes what occurs to him in his life. I began to realize that I had been writing second-person pieces all my life, but the poem that made me think of starting this book was "To the Unlikely Event." I thought I wanted them all to be unlikely—but of course the moment you want them all to be something, that becomes a form, and then they become likely [laughter], so that was impossible.

The unlikely event is something that everybody who has ever taken an airplane in our time has heard: "In the unlikely event of a water landing, your seat cushion can be used as a flotation device." [laughter] It's part of the incredible language that's been worked up. You don't get off an airplane, you "deplane," and "we *do* advise you to do such-and-such a thing." But again and again you can hear this sentence, "In the unlikely event . . ." in which the meaning of the language has been totally forgotten, and anyway nobody's listening.

So what is the unlikely event? Whatever happens next is the unlikely event, really. [laughter]

JW: No matter how much we anticipate it.

WSM: Yes, that's right.

JW: I wonder if you'd read another poem from *Present Company*, "To the Margin."

WSM:

To the Margin

Following the black
footprints the tracks
of words that have passed that way
before me I come
again and again to
your blank shore

not the end yet
but there is nothing more
to be seen there
to be read to be followed
to be understood
and each time I turn
back to go on
in the same way
that I draw the next breath

the wider you are
the emptier and the more
innocent of any
signal the more
precious the text
feels to me as I make
my way through it reminding
myself listening
for any sound from you

JW: Thank you. There's an extraordinary sense here of the presence of the lines disappearing into the absence of the right-hand margin. You write a number of poems in this book about language and words. I wonder if your sense of that kind of disappearance informs your thinking about the line.

WSM: Well, I suppose so. The line is a form. The line is also a unit of energy. Both of those things disappear—they disappear together in this case.

The line has gone through such mysterious changes just in our lifetimes, beginning with writers such as Pound, and particularly William Carlos Williams, and then Olson.

The phrase "free verse" is deceptive—there's no such thing as free verse. If a poem works, it *is* its form, and this is true whether it's in an abstractable form or whether it only happens once. What makes something a line has been shifting since one began to try to write things down. The line was clearly there in oral poetry, too, but there it was different. The line has to do, finally, with the *physical*. It may be very remote from its physical origins, but it's always there.

One of the things that disturbs me about a lot of recent poetry, undergraduate poetry, and people starting to write poetry at school for the first time—I have a feeling that they don't hear it at all. I have the feeling that writing on and looking at a computer all day has something to do with that. I don't know how poetry's going to survive that—I'm not quite sure that it will. I think it's going to make the distinction between prose and poetry more obvious, because poetry *won't* exist unless it's heard. If you don't hear it, there's no poetry there. If you've been reading a lot of students' poems you can begin to sift out quite quickly the ones who are *hearing* it and the ones who aren't. How do you say "you have to hear it . . ."? If the students don't hear it, they don't know what you mean.

JT: I have a follow-up question on "The Margin." You talk about "the signal" and the preciousness of the text. Do you have anything else you could say about that signal? For writers studying the craft of poetry, what are the signals that you're speaking of there?

WSM: Well, the line is not bearing any part of the meaning obviously in itself. It looks to be purely formal, and yet there's no such thing happening there. So that's what I mean by "innocent of any / signal." And yet all forms empower what they're the form *of*; they make it possible. If you take a sonnet of Shakespeare and write it out in prose, you begin to puzzle your head about all sorts of things that weren't puzzling before, because the form makes them clear. The form *is* an empowerment.

If you say this to students and they look baffled, they really don't have a sense of what poetry is yet, I think. When young children love poems, the form is really terribly important, even if it's a hopscotch rhyme. They know that without being able to say it.

JT: Because they hear the music—they hear the line, and they recognize the music of the line?

WSM: What the verse is saying and the form of saying it are the same. But that's true even with a poem which is clearly and apparently free verse, and it was true even when the haiku was written out as one line. It's always true. If a poem works, it's true.

JW: In *Present Company*, the poems look so casual on the page, and the voice is so intimate, that it's not immediately clear how formal the book is—more formal than any of your previous books, except perhaps your first one. I don't remember that you've depended on the sonnet form so much, or counted syllables and lines so much. It's interesting to hear what you say about form being a form of empowerment. What's driving your formal choices here, what do they empower, and what do they make difficult to express?

WSM: Well, I wanted it to be different—apparently different forms all the way through. Also, when you talk about the mixture of syllabics and metrical forms—this is something that's always been there, running through English. I can't speak to it in any other language because, although I have an acquaintance with other languages, I don't have the same intimate feeling for them, obviously, but I think there's been a kind of ambivalence built into English prosody right from the beginning. We think of iambic pentameter as the basic meter of English, but it's not. Iambic pentameter is a meter imported in Chaucer's time from Italy, via France, but it's not a French meter either. It's basically an Italian meter, but by the time you get it into English it's not like the Italian meter. We know what the English meter is based on—the meter of Middle English, which goes back into Anglo-Saxon. It's based on rowing. The people who used it developed it out of chants from rowing, and the break in the middle is the break in between the drawing and the return of the oar, back and forth.

JW: That's the caesura.

WSM: That's the caesura. The English meter isn't metrical in the same sense as the iambic pentameter. It counts only the stressed syllables; it's a syllabic meter. The Italian sonnet has some of the same ambivalence, too, because the Classical meter—the Roman or Latin meter—is a stressed meter; it's not a straight eleven-syllable line like the Italian meter. So there's this play back and forth, and I think this play is essential. When you get too rigid one way or the other, when you get too committed to doing it one way or the other, the meter goes dead. It becomes a dead convention, and very boring. You can go into great tracts of iambic pentameter in the nineteenth century and think, "Oh my God, this is so dull." One of the reasons is that that play, that pull in different directions, isn't there. Pope understood this very well. Pope was one of the two or three strictest users of the iambic pentameter in English. Students are not brought up able to hear Pope, so they think he's very boring. But if you listen to Pope, he's not boring—he's a brilliant, brilliant poet. The variation of cadence and tempo in Pope is absolutely endless, and it's very subtle. He *heard* it. He certainly heard it very, very well. And in each one of his longer poems, he heard it differently.

JW: I want to go back to an earlier point in your career. A lot has been made in the critical literature about the transition in your work starting with *The Moving Target* (1963)[2] in the 1960s, but it seems to me that there was another watershed in your writing after *The Rain in the Trees* (1988),[3] beginning in the 1990s, when you returned to the kind of formalism of your earlier books, and long narrative poems that really had no precedent in your work before began to appear. I wonder if you could say something about what allowed you so thoroughly to revise your style at that point.

WSM: The assumption is that all this is planned in advance. But it's much more a sense of coming to the feeling that I've done what I wanted to do in that direction, and that the open ground is already somewhere else, and it's important to change it. The worst possible thing would be to start trying to do something you've already done. That's spinning your wheels.

JW: Did you feel like you had come to the end of a certain kind of thing with *The Rain in the Trees*?

WSM: Yes. But I would say anything like that with real caution, because this is true for *me*. I'm not saying that this is a prescription for other people. Andrew Marvell basically wrote in much the same form, same tone, and same meter all his life. So did Jean Follain, in French. For some poets that's the way to do it, you know, and for some musicians that's the way to do it. If the poet is really good, you see great changes within a single form, and that's admirable. Look at somebody like Auden. He really did change enormously from his early poems—which, by the way, I admire very much, I think they're very, very brilliant—to the late poems. But his poems are always extremely and obviously and abstractly formal. He said once, with the false modesty that Auden was very good at, that he didn't feel confident about writing without formal structure, that he would have felt lost immediately if he had done it. But then he also said he thought he'd written in every meter that was known in English, and it was probably true.

JT: I'd like to ask you about the collection *The Vixen* (1996),[4] centering on two things. First, how *The Vixen* is a book that evokes a place, that's so much *of* the place, and second, how the structure of these poems seems to be a kind of enjambed statement. I believe Richard Howard is the one who coined that phrase in a book review. Rather than lines per se, as we've been talking about, the poems in *The Vixen* operate with a kind of an engine of an enjambed statement. In reading these poems, I feel that there's tremendous energy in that form. I've spent a lot of time looking at them and trying to take them apart and understand that, but it's sort of intuitive. I can't really get my hands around a form per se. Is there anything you can say about that?

WSM: That's good, that's good. [laughter] I would like that to be so. I know how the book began, which is probably not an answer, but it's a direction for an answer to your question. It began with the first poem ["Fox Sleep"], which is quite different from the rest of the book, because it's a five-part poem. It's specifically about the vixen, but it's about different ways of coming to the vixen, whoever the vixen is. Also, I hope it would dispose of the idea of treating the vixen as a symbol. The vixen is more complicated than a symbol. The vixen is an appearing and disappearing presence that is there all the time. I wasn't thinking about writing a series of poems, but when I finished that first one, I wanted to go on to the next one and the next one and the next one. I realized that this is the vixen, you know, that this is where the vixen goes.

I do have a strong feeling of the fox as a spirit animal. I think this is true in our karmic relations with the natural world altogether. I really think there's a connection between the horrors of World War II and several centuries of horrible mistreatment of foxes in the British Isles. Siegfried Sassoon suggested it in *Memoirs of a Fox-Hunting Man*. He doesn't mean to, but I think that's one of the things that comes through. The attitude to the world that's there in fox hunting . . . there's no reason to hunt foxes, except that they get in the way of our raising chickens. We want to eat the chickens, and they want to, and damn it, what are *they* doing there? We put fifty of them together, which never happens in the natural world, and then we get mad at them because they eat fifty instead of one. You can understand people getting angry with foxes, but if you then go ahead and demonize them the way we've done, you cease to be able to see them. They're amazing because they're one of the rare wild animals who are really interested in us, constantly interested in us. We don't know what the base of that interest is, so they know something about us that we don't know.

JT: In the poem "Vixen," you speak to the vixen as if she were something that has come to you and left you and come back to you, and you're seeking this spirit as an affirmation of life, of writing, of something. It seems very personal to you, not just historical, as you were just saying. It seems to the speaker that the vixen is a totem animal.

WSM: I think so. I didn't know that to begin with. The vixen who is evoked in the first poem, in "Fox Sleep"—all that is historically true, and it's both the vixen and the *place* that go and return. The vixen becomes the kind of spirit of the place, and still is for me. What the future of that is I don't know, in my life or in the world. But the vixen certainly is the "wild" that Thoreau was talking about. Thoreau didn't say "In wilderness is the preservation of the world"; he said, "In *wildness* is the preservation of the world." Wildness does not simply mean a place where you don't have all-terrain vehicles. It means that deepest and most precious aspect of our lives, which we can never get our fingers around, which we can never possess, can never follow, can never grasp, and yet it's always there.

JT: It's always impelling us forward.

WSM: Yes, it's the most precious thing we have. And everybody has it.

JT: Does that somehow play in with the energy in these lines, these statements? Is that where the energy's coming from?

WSM: Well, I *hope* so. But there's also another source of that: the stone mill fox that was the beginning of the whole thing, this stone mill in the form of a fox, apparently asleep. When I wanted to write the poem, the form that suggested itself—which has to do also with age and with time passing and all of that—was an elegiac form, the form that derives from the Roman elegy, which indeed is not a metrical form. It's a syllabic form, a stressed form. It's a form that follows its stresses. I haven't ever counted them, but I think that most of the lines in "Fox Sleep" have basically the same number of stresses. They're not at all the same number of syllables. That makes something you can hear, and that you can expect.

That's another link between the prosody of verse and something like the presence of a fox. The prosody of verse, if it doesn't put you to sleep, sets up an expectation and never quite fulfills it. It always keeps changing. If you get a straight iambic pentameter line over and over again, even if it's something that has to be sung . . . if you have it absolutely straight, it will put you to sleep. It's dull. You can't hear it. So the prosody of verse sets up an expectation and then keeps eluding you. Very important, I think. Very important for the form of verse altogether. Does that make sense?

JT: Yes, it makes total sense, and we could talk a long time about this. But I'd like to switch gears just a little bit here. Although we're all very interested in form and content and structure, I'd like to touch on political poetry for just a minute. In the 1960s, you were very involved in writing about the war. And everyone is very familiar with your poems about the environment. Today, we have a situation where writers have the opportunity to choose either to write about what's happening in the world or to turn their faces away from it. I wonder if you have anything you'd like to say to these writers about political poetry.

WSM: It's an endless topic, because you can't really ever say anything definitive about it. The obvious thing is that most political poetry is very bad. That's no reason for not writing it—most love poetry is very bad too. We don't know how to write love poems. But the fascinating thing, I think, is *why* it's bad. Most love poetry is bad because the feeling is a sort of a bully that insists on being the dictator of the whole thing from beginning to end. That didn't happen with Shakespeare. Shakespeare knew what he was doing. You don't know anything about Shakespeare's love life—you recognize it because it's something you recognize from your *own* life.

It's not that there aren't any good political poems. One of the great political poems you can think of immediately is *The Divine Comedy*. It is quite possible to write great political poems, but only if they evolve in the same way and come from the same places that any other real poem comes from. In other words, if they come out of the fact that you are right, and that you have the right opinion about this and you're just going to show other people what the right opinion is, you're going to have a piece of propaganda. It may be brilliant propaganda, but it's going to be short-lived and in the long run boring—maybe in the short run boring, too. To say where a poem must come from to make it a real poem is impossible, as we know. But we know when it's true and when it isn't. When political writing comes from the same imaginative source that makes any other kind of poetry real and good, then you can get a good poem. It doesn't happen very often.

Not all the poems written during the time of the Vietnam War were bad. Some of them were wonderful. Denise Levertov must have written dozens and dozens of poems about the Vietnam War that you don't remember at all anymore, but there are two or three that are quite wonderful. They were unlikely. One or two of them would be about some detail of Vietnam that had vanished or something like that, and you suddenly focus on something very specific that maybe is completely imaginary, and yet it touches the feeling of loss, the feeling of jeopardy, the feeling of waste, the feeling of unnecessary and mendacious destruction that we all feel at the moment.

I think about this appalling thing that we're all implicated in and deplore, halfway around the world. At the moment, one of the things that I think is frustrating and infuriating is that it seems to be very hard to say anything about it, far more so than in the Vietnam War. You get very little writing about it, very little poetry, very little singing—none of that. The Vietnam War came at the same time as a groundswell of opposition to many, many things in the society. It's as though that groundswell of opposition isn't there at the moment. There's far more acceptance of the details of the world, the social details of the world around us, than there was then. It was a real rejection. It wasn't deep enough, it hadn't got its roots down, it got destroyed by the Chicago convention, the wind all went out of it, but it was *there*, and it did make for confrontations like Kent State and finally the march on the Pentagon and things like that. Nothing like that's in the wind right now. Why, I don't know. That's the difference between the two times. Another difference is that the imaginative articulation in songs and poems . . . I don't see them, I don't hear them.

JT: Thank you. We have a few minutes to entertain some follow-up questions from the audience.

Q: Why do you think that we're not seeing an imaginative articulation about this war? It's really disturbing to me that we're not. Where's Bob Dylan?

WSM: Well, it's a very good question. I don't know. Insofar as I have any notion of it at all—and I distrust it because I'm farther away from it than I was at that time . . . I was spending a lot of time in New York and in other cities at that time, much more than I am now, and feeling more involved with New York, which for me, rightly or wrongly and for better or worse, was the center of history. I felt closer to it then, but there was a preparation for it. My suspicion, insofar as I've got a theory about it, is that it has to with the media. Kids play in the street far less, they spend more time watching television. Kids grow up spending less time running around in the woods and more time playing computer games. And I think these things may lead to a kind of remoteness from direct experience of other kinds, including social ones. I regret it, but I regret many things happening in the world, and I don't know what to . . .

Q: You mean learning to imagine? Is that what you're talking about?

WSM: Do you think that's possible? I think that the imagination is a sensual thing. It's not an abstract thing. It has to do with hearing. It has to do with seeing and smelling and touching. It has to do with the senses, it comes out of the senses. If you have sensory deprivation, the imagination stops. I think that if you spend all of your time watching a play of images on a screen, which you have nothing to do with except to sit there and watch it . . . I got told things like this when I was growing up: "I don't think it's good for you." [laughs]

Q: This is really just a comment. I wanted to thank you for saying that a poem that takes a form becomes a form of its own. That's something that I've said forever and been argued with. But now I can say, "Well, if W. S. Merwin says it . . ." [laughter] That's important. It's something I've always believed, and it's the first time I've ever heard anyone say it.

Q: You said that although you were familiar with foreign languages, you were most comfortable with English. In your translations of Neruda, I was just wondering how you were able to capture the nuances. I was wondering, if you weren't familiar with Spanish, how you were able to write those poems.

WSM: Oh, I didn't mean that I was not familiar with it, but I mean that the kind of intimacy that I have with English, in which . . . if you set up fifteen phrases which would all theoretically express the same thing—of course they don't—I hear immediately the one that is the right one, or seems to me the right one. I may not be nearly that clear about it even in a language that

I've had familiarity with for many years, like Spanish or French. Sometimes if I know the poem by memory it begins to be clear, but it's not nearly as clear. I just don't hear it, and if it were read out loud I wouldn't hear it that clearly either.

Q: I have a question about revision. How many of your poems land on the page and stay that way, I'm curious to know.

WSM: I can think of only one in my whole life. [laughs]

Q: So you do have to go through the revision process?

WSM: Usually I can't separate writing from revision. I'm turning it until it gets where I really want it to stop. It never stops turning. I don't know why anyone would want manuscripts of mine to study, because they're completely illegible. Everything is written on top of everything else, and nobody can ever begin to figure out the sequence of choices, even if they could read them.

Q: I think a lot of people think that to be a writer you should get it right the first time. We all want to feel that way.

WSM: No, but very often when people say that . . . if they know enough, the example that they cite is preliterate poetry—American Indian lyrics, the few that we have, or Eskimo poetry where someone stood up and said the poem, as if it happened like that. They may have been sitting there for nine or ten or eleven months chewing this thing over before they stood up and said it. People have said, about the haiku of Bashō, "Bashō just wrote it down like that." Yes, he did, but he may have spent years thinking about it, getting it right.

Millennial Merwin

Sarah Kennedy

In late December 1999, I was driving to Vermont from Virginia, leaving Petersburg in an ice storm that had snapped off trees and power lines all the way up I-95. I still had electricity, but I was apprehensive about leaving my computer (at that time a big old desktop, too unwieldy to pack), because I wouldn't be back until mid-January 2000. The possibility of a power surge was part of my nervousness; I was also concerned that the machine wouldn't make the millennial turn on New Year's Day. I had to go, though, so I plugged in a surge protector, shrugged, and pulled the door shut on the problem.

The problem, of course, never emerged. I returned to a melted, puddly Virginia and a working computer. Everyone on my floor at school was laughing and trading stories about the lengths they had gone to in preparing for a crisis that never materialized. The new millennium looked benign, and we carried on as though we had passed the worst.

What does any of this have to do with reading W. S. Merwin? As the new century began with the onslaught of the George W. Bush election and presidency, then the attacks of 9/11, I felt that poets would have to respond to the political world in direct ways. And they did, of course. I did too. W. S. Merwin did as well, having been all his career one of the most philosophically and politically thoughtful and careful poets writing in the English language.

And yet when I read Merwin's work published since 2000, I find his approaches more subtle than those of many of us who tackled the world about us. What feels in the hands of lesser poets like a tire iron Merwin uses with the delicacy of a fine paintbrush, showing a narrator who is also thinking about time and people and landscapes.

I go back to *The Pupil*, published in 2001.[1] Obviously, many of the poems in this collection were written before the turn of the century. What I find, however, is a meditation on darkness, on shadow, and on song—birdsong, echo—oftentimes rising out of that shade, and I seem to be reading a poet who foresaw the last decade's catastrophes with more clarity and more sorrow than many others. The first poem in the collection, in fact, is titled "Prophecy," and its subject is a singing sibyl whom "no one hears." This poem ends with an image of a "light coming from far out in the eye" that is going to burn "through the words that no one has believed." Now, I wouldn't want to read too much into this poem politically, but the mood of "Prophecy" catches, for me, much of what has happened in public speech since 9/11.

The prevalence of poems in darkness in this collection astonishes me. Even titles—"The Time of Shadow," "The Hours of Darkness," "Flights in the Dark," "Migrants by Night"—suggest a preoccupation that speaks to the larger conditions of our millennial world. I don't mean this in a simplistic or deterministic way; I don't mean to say that Merwin became a prophet of doom casting jeremiads over the Pacific. His poems have always been embedded in contemporary culture, including politics, war, violence, and injustice. And Merwin is himself aging, the poems becoming increasingly interested in reflection, memory, even nostalgia, both wistful and melancholy. The implications of his work since 2001, however, seem to me to reach further into sadness, to draw it out metaphorically and imagistically into language.

The poems about song and music in *The Pupil* are not invariably gloomy; they do, however, usually locate the most beautiful sounds in the past or in the dark. "The Time of Shadow" is typical in this regard. The entire poem is cast as a sort of reverie on loss; generations of people are shadows, and images of lost sound dominate: "the choir loft in the church burned long ago" and "the sounds of mourning / . . . for the whole loss without a name." The poem ends with the hope that there may come a time when there will be "singing again out of the dark trees," but no sign of when that might happen. "One Night in April" begins in silence and ends with a memory of "two notes" once heard that are now "maybe a thousand / miles on their way / northward over / the dark of the ocean," that are, for the speaker, "now too far / tonight to hear." In "Unknown Bird," the brief "fluted phrase" is present but so distant that it "is gone before it / goes on fallen into / its own echo."

Merwin's deft touch with image prevents these poems from becoming maudlin or self-pitying. The owl that wakes at night and "says it is summer" in "First of June," and then seeks out whose "turn it is tonight to be changed," is doing what owls are supposed to do—find prey and eat what they must to stay alive. Humans are the beings who make of song a senselessly violent melody, such as the "chords" in "Overtone" that become, for some listeners at a concert, the echo of "music played during a war." But Merwin speaks, as he so often does, of humanity at large, which includes the speaker but does not focus exclusively on him; all of us are implicated in the neglect of the natural world which leads to the neglect, and finally the destruction, of the environment that sustains us. We are, in "Unknown Bird," the worst kind of predators, "foreign" to the birds, and silencing them so that we may fill "the days / with a sound of our own."

We like to think of ourselves as enlightened creatures, but *The Pupil*, with its pun on the eye (which should allow comprehension, vision) and the student (who should be open to the light of learning) gives the lie to our self-satisfied assumptions. Easy assignments of meaning to those old metaphors of dark and light are twisted beyond recognition at the end of "The Marfa Lights," where

> in the eye of the mind where we know
> from the beginning that the darkness
> is beyond us there is no explaining
> the dark it is only the light
> that we keep feeling a need to account for

Merwin published *Present Company* in 2005.[2] I read through it almost ferociously, hungry for a vision of the world and of human beings that would elevate me to a place where I could come to terms with, or at least make some larger sense of, the wars started by the United States government in Afghanistan and Iraq. Pat Tillman had been killed by his fellow soldiers, and I had students of my own going off to fight who had joined the National Guard or one of the branches of the military as a way of covering tuition. They hoped to have solid, respectable, dependable incomes and careers, and military service seemed to answer all their needs.

In one creative writing class, I had a student who was between tours of duty; she was using the semester to add some credits toward her undergraduate degree and to decide whether she would sign on again. This student was not an English major and didn't have much desire to write poems; she needed three hours of humanities and experiential credit for college, and the course fit those requirements. She was quiet, almost withdrawn, and sat with her seatback pushed against a side wall, a part of the circle but as far to its edge as possible. Her work dealt with her job in the military: to clean up bodies as much as possible before they were returned to grieving relatives. The poems were graphic, horrific, and tremendously sad, and when, at the end of the semester, she asked me to write her a letter of recommendation when she enlisted for another tour (I still don't know why she needed a letter from me), I gently but firmly refused. She seemed damaged enough. Maybe it was a selfish decision, but I simply couldn't bring myself to write something that would help her get back into that place.

I wanted her to stay home and write more poems, however "good" or "bad" they were. And one of the books I gave her that semester was *Present Company*, because its elegiac tone—the poems are all apostrophes to various things, ideas, and absent people—seemed necessary for every American to experience and share. These are poems of loss and anger, even as rage at our human ability to destroy is tempered by Merwin's characteristic wisdom and compassion. The short sequence of dated poems, written in the days after the attacks on the World Trade Center and the Pentagon, seemed especially important to me; they are lovely and horrifying at the same time. The last of this series, "To the Coming Winter," was a poem I had the entire class read, both for its formal excellence as a sonnet and for its ability to speak about public and private matters simultaneously. The ending lines, "we stand watching / those brief flares in the silence of heaven / without knowing what they are signaling," made some of the students weep.

But my soldier did not cry. She seldom showed any emotion. And the last I heard, she had gone back to Iraq to serve again.

I put three poems from *Present Company* on my door: "To _____," "To the Consolations of Philosophy," and "To Grief." Even more than the September 2001 poems, these seemed to me the best expressions of what could be felt about our country and our species in those days. Here's "To _____":

> There is no reason
> for me to keep counting
> how long it has been
> since you were here
> alive one morning
>
> as though I were
> letting out the string
> of a kite one day at a time
> over my finger
> when there is no string

I never saw that student again and I confess I can no longer remember her name. What I do recall, over and over, are the first two lines of "To the Consolations of Philosophy": "Thank you but / not just at the moment."

The Shadow of Sirius, published in 2008, seems now, as does so much of Merwin's work, prophetic.[3] Autumn of that year was chaotic. I was in Scotland that fall, and I watched the news of the stock market's crash from my Edinburgh hotel room. David Foster Wallace committed suicide, and the papers both in the north and in London carried full-page spreads on his life and work. Barack Obama was elected too, however, and the hope generated by that success wrenched the news in the other direction. Many of my friends, and I, hoped that the wars would soon end and the economy would glitch and go forward.

But the wars continued. The economy faltered, continues to falter, and I returned to the United States to find my students in financial crises as their parents lost jobs and the ability to send them to college. The military looked more and more like the solution to their immediate problems as well as their long-term fears about employment. I kept teaching poetry, wondering for the first time whether I was doing them a favor by insisting that the right word in the right place could make a difference to them as human beings.

The Shadow of Sirius is unexpectedly (at least to me) largely about light. Merwin seldom writes literally or directly about isolated contemporary events, but this book spoke to me in ways that made a grim sense as the first decade of the new millennium wound to its end. The registers of language that we often expect to find together—light, enlightenment, identification, naming—are broken in these poems into sparkling shards that say more of loss and destruction than they do of gain, economic or moral. In the daytime of these late poems, what we can see is the result of our errors; the moments of joy are small and immediate and priceless.

"By the Avenue" takes on the contemporary world most directly. It begins with a long view, "through the trees and across the river," but the image soon turns sinister. The water is "the color of steel," and the narrator is revealed to be looking at "the splintered skyline of the city." The city is never identified, but does it matter? The speaker feels that he is the "only one who can / remember now . . . / the young leaves brighter than the daylight," a sense we all have as we age and watch the cities of our youth change. This brief sonnetlike poem ends with a personal memory of a father's voice "telling about a mote in an eye / that was like a mote in a sunbeam." It's a lovely ending, but it also contains a warning note; a mote in the eye alters perception, distorts what is seen. It is a flaw in vision, and it refers to us all.

Absence figures largely in these late poems, as it does in much of Merwin's work. "The Silence of the Mine Canaries" contains no canaries at all, and perhaps that is the point. The poem is about the flying creatures that have gone missing: bats, swallows, robins, blue tits, cuckoos, nightjars, thrushes, blackcaps. After this long catalog, the speaker remembers having seen and heard all of them when he was young without realizing their significance. He ends by stating that "they were singing of youth / not knowing that they were singing for us." If the birds are unaware of this, however, then the youth they must have been singing for was their own. This brings me back to the title. Mine canaries fall silent when the air has become poisonous. They die as a warning to humans that the environment is hazardous. The title now reveals itself as emblematic of our relationship to the environment at large—we are destroying it, and the absence of birds ought to be a warning to us. But whether we are sensitive enough to hear that caution is another matter.

Sadly, the answer seems to be no, and Merwin's late work seems to know it. The poems in *The Shadow of Sirius* are beautiful and mournful, unwilling to give up hope in the face of our inability to imagine a world beyond war and economic upheaval. Still, the note of sadness runs through the book, and the light is often on the verge of going out. "Rain Light" remembers the speaker's mother telling him that he will be "all right," that the flowers "wake without a question / even though the whole world is burning." In "Lights Out," it is already full dark:

> The old grieving autumn goes on calling to its summer
> the valley is calling to other valleys beyond the ridge
> each star is roaring alone into darkness
> there is not a sound in the whole night

Now, it might be asked why we need melancholy poems in recession-ridden, war-conscious contemporary America. Don't we want happy poems, funny poems, poems to make us feel better about ourselves and our country? Well, maybe. But then I go back to that morning when I left for Vermont, driving through the ice storm toward what I was sure would be a brighter future. And I was right—briefly. But the passing of that short and spectacular storm and the hyperbole of the catastrophists at the turn of the millennium were nothing, really, compared to what was to come—and as a metaphor it now seems like the monsters of youth. It was not our technology we needed to fear: it was ourselves. The computers kept working, but our ability to make use of them to improve communication and thought did not. And now we find ourselves at war, out of work, and scrambling to explain to our students why studying literature should be important to them. And again I turn to Merwin, who speaks to us with a wisdom—not despairing but instructive—that we would do well to heed:

> The late poems are the ones
> I turn to first now
> following a hope that keeps

beckoning me
waiting somewhere in the lines
almost in plain sight

it is the late poems
that are made of words
that have come the whole way
they have been there

The Shadow of Sirius
A Critical Conversation

Mark Halliday and Michael Theune

Introduction / Michael Theune

One of the features that make Cary Nelson and Ed Folsom's *W. S. Merwin: Essays on the Poetry,* published in 1987, such a significant collection is its willingness to present both positive and negative views of Merwin's work. In the book's introduction, Folsom and Nelson state their belief that this approach is simply accurate, reflecting the critical debate arising in reviews of Merwin's works, which "have . . . been the site of much disputation."[1] Attempting to incorporate more of "the context of contemporary debate" and to downplay the inevitable "idealizations of the canon," Folsom and Nelson state that they tried to create "a combination of positive and negative essays, making a collection that thereby gives extended treatment to the issues shaping contemporary debate on Merwin's work."[2]

Our work in this critical conversation is a condensation of this approach. Here we will engage in a dispute over the value of Merwin's 2008 book of poems, *The Shadow of Sirius*: I will argue, in the first, third, and fifth sections of the exchange, the case for the book's value, and Mark will argue, in the second and fourth sections, against it.[3] In fact, by containing the poem "Worn Words," *The Shadow of Sirius* virtually calls for this kind of analysis. In "Worn Words" Merwin writes of the way in which he now privileges late poems, stating that "[t]he late poems are the ones / I turn to first now." Merwin privileges these poems because "it is the late poems / that are made of words / that have come the whole way / they have been there." So: what can the late poems of W. S. Merwin, poems "that have come the whole way," tell us? Do they have anything new to say or to reveal? Are the poems in *The Shadow of Sirius* accomplished, and, if so, what do they accomplish? What, if anything, does this late book have to show us about Merwin's craft and career? What, if anything, does it say about the trajectory of and tendencies in American poetry?

We will try, in the course of our conversation, to address these questions, even while heeding the warnings of Folsom and Nelson, who state that "the politics, the rhetoric, the stresses, the ambitions, and the delusions built into literary evaluation are particularly evident in evaluating our contemporaries, where judgments are strikingly theatrical and unstable."[4] By engaging in dialogue, we hope to avoid excessive theatricality, each serving, at varying times, as the other's sounding board, collaborator, and critic.

Before we attempt our different assessments of Merwin's 2008 book, I would like to simply describe it. *The Shadow of Sirius* is a book of, generally, very compact lyric poems. Of its ninety-three poems, only eleven exceed one page, and none exceeds two pages. The book contains three sections, consisting of twenty-eight, eleven, and fifty-four poems, respectively. And these sections are grouped, to a large extent, thematically. The first section focuses on memory, along with its attendant absences and the presences— the triggers, the associations, and even, literally, the mnemonic devices, including music, musical instruments, archives, inherited objects, keepsakes, and ancient texts—that recall those absences. The poems in this section include numerous meditations on the past and the dead, and the ways they are called up, brought forth. Recalling that Sirius is the "Dog Star," the second section—dedicated "in memory of Muku, Makana, Koa"—consists mainly of recollections of and elegies for Merwin's dogs, and poems that employ the dog as a figure both for death and a persistent hope for future possibility. The third and largest section is more difficult to pin down in terms of thematic content. Many of the poems seem to feature a return to Merwin's home in southwestern France, and a number of others involve travel, distance, disappearance, return, and the paradoxical, constantly fluctuating relationship between absence and presence.

Though *The Shadow of Sirius* contains late poems, it would be a mistake to think that they encapsulate or summarize Merwin's whole career. At least one key element from the trajectory of Merwin's career is largely missing from *The Shadow of Sirius*: clear engagement with political concerns. And this, of course, is not negligible when one considers, on the one hand, how vital to Merwin's career were the apocalyptic poems of *The Lice* (1967), including "The Asians Dying" and "For a Coming Extinction," and, on the other hand, the political events—including wars in Iraq and Afghanistan, the revelation that the United States government condoned torture—occurring during the time the poems in *The Shadow of Sirius* were being written. There are moments of political concern in *The Shadow of Sirius*. But these are only a few instances—a few poems and a few lines—in a book of ninety-three poems. There is, for example, no poem called "The Iraqi Civilians Dying."

So what does this leave us with? What do Merwin's late poems reveal?

I / Michael Theune

With its interest in "late poems," "Worn Words" makes me think of Edward Said's notion of "late style." Said defines two styles of lateness. One style, embodied in the late work of Beethoven and Adorno, is characterized by "a nonharmonious, nonserene tension, and, above all, a sort of deliberatively unproductive productiveness going *against*."[5] In the other style, embodied in works such as Shakespeare's *The Tempest* and *The Winter's Tale* and Sophocles's *Oedipus at Colonus*, "[w]e meet the accepted notion of age and wisdom in some last works that reflect a special maturity, a new spirit of reconciliation and serenity often expressed in terms of a miraculous transfiguration of common reality."[6]

Of the two late styles, Merwin most closely adheres to the second, the style of serene acceptance and reconciliation. However, I would like to suggest that in *The Shadow of Sirius* Merwin exemplifies another style of lateness: a super-serene one from an author who long ago discovered a late style that was invested in "a miraculous transfiguration of common reality" and remains in that state, in that style. This super-serene becomes most apparent when one recognizes that numerous poems in *The Shadow of Sirius* uncover new layers of absence in which both the past and the signs of the past are missing. Although one assumes that the accumulation of such losses could be traumatic, Merwin does not seem especially affected by them. For example, in "Lament for a Stone," Merwin mourns losing a stone he had kept from a visit to the beach where St. Columba landed after leaving Ireland. Though lost, the memento remains efficacious: in the course of the poem, Merwin still seems able to successfully remember that shore. There certainly are moments of grief and despair in *The Shadow of Sirius*, but, as with the book's political content, these moments are very rare and relatively quickly overcome.

While one might wish for Merwin to explore such difficult feelings more fully, he does not. Merwin—we can see it plainly now—is not a poet of such unruliness, such unsuccessful mourning; rather, he is a poet of great equilibrium and poise. Merwin also is a great poet, and *The Shadow of Sirius* is a fine book that reveals something persistent in his work but not fully articulated by those who have commented on it: that Merwin is much less concerned with offering a particular political opinion or formulating a system, and much more concerned with creating poems. He once stated, "I've no principle against political poems. I just wish, sometimes desperately, that mine or anyone else's turned out more often to be poetry."[7] And what Merwin means by "poetry" is deeply involved with the creation of surprise. I want to think here about one of the key—but, so far, under-recognized—means by which Merwin crafts surprise.

Surprise is vital to Merwin. In a 1947 letter to Ezra Pound, he offers the reason he prefers *Personae* to *The Cantos,* claiming that there is more "sheer poetic magic" in *Personae,* and he defines poetic magic as "that element of perpetual and delicious surprise."[8] And surprise is a key element of Merwin's poems. In "Reading Merwin Semiotically," Robert Scholes, who states that a semiotic reading, in part, views the poem as "achieving poetic status by violating certain kinds of expectation,"[9] reads three earlier poems by Merwin and shows how they all deliver (often multiple) surprises. In a discussion of some earlier poems, H. L. Hix notes that these poems employ myth "as a set of expectations to subvert."[10] Merwin is even explicit in some of his poems about the value of surprise. In "To Dido," what the poem is made out of, or what the poem is, is in part "a still place of perpetual surprise,"[11] while Merwin's "The Blind Seer of Ambon" concludes, "[E]verything takes me by surprise / it is all awake in the darkness."[12]

The source of many of the surprises and the technique for surprise-making in Merwin's poems often is a *turning*. Much has been made of the fact that Merwin has a very set poetic vocabulary. For example, Thomas B. Byers notes that he deploys a particular set of "disembodied icons," including "doors, birds, glass, clouds, eyes, hair, ash, dust, statues, wings, water, stone, feet, bells, fire, veins."[13] Most of the lists drawn up of Merwin's word-talismans are lists of nouns, of things. However, were one to include in these lists verbs he deploys, *turn* would definitely make the cut. The verb *turn* and versions of it (*turns, turned, turning*—not to mention all the versions of the word *return*) are conspicuously present in his poetry.[14]

Turning has multiple meanings for Merwin. For the Buddhist Merwin, turning is an essential part of the transient, ever-changing world, and as such it is the subject of a great number of his poems. Additionally, his poems turn both formally and structurally. Merwin's poems, like virtually all poems, turn at the end of each line to the beginning of the next line—it is precisely this movement that allows poetry to be called verse. The significance of the formal turn, however, is perhaps clearer in Merwin's poems than in many other poems because the absence of punctuation creates no other obvious breaks in the line. Much has been made of his unpunctuated lines—perhaps to the detriment of discussion of another kind of turning in his poems—so I'll not focus on them here. Rather, I want to consider how Merwin's poems also turn *structurally*—that is, how they engage major shifts in their rhetorical or dramatic trajectory. Consider "The Long and the Short of It":

> As long as we can believe anything
> we believe in measure
> we do it with the first breath we take
> and the first sound we make
> it is in each word we learn
> and in each of them it means
> what will come again and when
> it is there in *meal* and in *moon*
> and in *meaning* it is the meaning
> it is the firmament and the furrow

> turning at the end of the field
> and the verse turning with its breath
> it is in memory that keeps telling us
> some of the old story about us

Occurring at the beginning of a line, the "turning" in line 11 clearly refers to the formal turning that takes place at each of the poem's line breaks, the poem's "verse turning." However, though less obviously, "The Long and the Short of It"—a poem that, with fourteen lines, resembles the sonnet—also contains the structural turn of its volta. "The Long and the Short of It" opens by arguing that language is not merely language but also all that comes along with it when we learn it, including the constant measure of breath. This opening moves the poem toward its turn (at the end of line 8): the revelation that these existential facts are the deep "meaning" of language. The rest of the poem then tries to represent this deep meaning. Though the two references to turning in this short poem point primarily to formal turning, it is important to recognize that they also both occur after, and so point back to, the poem's most significant volta. That is, Merwin uses a variation on the word *turn* to self-consciously highlight a structural turn.[15]

Merwin is widely recognized as a formal master; it's important to see that he is also a master of the structural turn. Though they haven't made the point as directly as I have, two very different critics, Helen Vendler and Marjorie Perloff, both recognize Merwin's tendency to turn and skill with turning. In her review of *The Shadow of Sirius*, Vendler sees "One of the Butterflies" and "Youth in Grass" as sonnets even though formally the poems—of thirteen and fifteen lines, respectively—are not sonnets. Still, each acts like a sonnet: each contains a structural turn, a volta. Of "One of the Butterflies," Vendler notes, "I could print these thirteen lines as a quasi-sonnet . . . thereby suggesting its European lineage and its division into a problem (the timing of pleasure) and a conclusion (its elusiveness past and present)."[16] Vendler describes "Youth in Grass" as "a fifteen-line sonnet-like meditation . . . on the rapidity with which . . . a year turns from spring to autumn."[17] She states, "The most salient aspect of the Merwin mind in meditation is its tenacity to its perplexity. Nothing can interrupt it once it has located its chosen difficulty—whether in perception, in thought, in human relations, or in memory."[18] I think Vendler's insight is accurate; I would only add that a major part of Merwin's tenacity is the accomplishment of the turn.

In her own way, Marjorie Perloff makes a similar case. In her 1987 essay "Apocalypse Then: Merwin and the Sorrows of Literary History," she critiques the notion that Merwin's work might accurately be described by "phrases like 'prophecy' or 'negative mysticism' or 'naked poetry' or 'the opening of the field.'"[19] Instead, Perloff makes the case that Merwin's poetry "carried on the tradition of the well-made poem," a poem marked by "authorial control."[20] She consistently roots Merwin's authorial control in structural control, in the management of turns. For example, she initiates her examination of the "strong sense of closure" in "For the Anniversary of My Death" by discussing the structural motion of the poem: "The first stanza (five lines) describes what happens 'Every year'; the second (eight lines) refers to 'Then' (when I will be dead)."[21] Further on in her analysis, Perloff makes the case that "[t]he poem's closure is reflected in its formal verse structure."[22] She concludes, "'For the Anniversary of My Death' is thus a very elegant, well-made poem; it has a finish that would be the envy of any number of poets."[23]

The Shadow of Sirius contains many surprising turns. Indeed, once one has come to recognize the presence of the turn in Merwin's poetry, a great deal of the pleasure of reading his work derives from the anticipation of seeing where the poem will go, what it will turn into. This certainly is the case with "Youth":

> Through all of youth I was looking for you
> without knowing what I was looking for
>
> or what to call you I think I did not
> even know I was looking how would I
>
> have known you when I saw you as I did
> time after time when you appeared to me
>
> as you did naked offering yourself
> entirely at that moment and you let

me breathe you touch you taste you knowing
no more than I did and only when I

began to think of losing you did I
recognize you when you were already

part memory part distance remaining
mine in the ways that I learn to miss you

from what we cannot hold the stars are made

"Youth" begins with a mystery: who is the "you," and did the speaker find the "you"? But instead of pursuing the identity of the "you," the poem turns into a playful acknowledgment of epistemological paradox: the speaker, it turns out, has known the "you" very well, but it is just this closeness—perhaps combined with youthful naiveté (on the part, potentially, of both the I and the you: Merwin's lack of punctuation allows this possibility in the lines "you knowing / no more than I did")—that prevents the speaker from knowing. Distance, it turns out, is necessary for knowledge, or at least memory, with its illusions of possession.

At this point, the poem already ingeniously contains two possible readings. On the one hand, it is a poem about a relationship the speaker recalls with a specific other (or others), a lover (or lovers) from one's youth—and the poem captures so much of the unknowingness of these early relationships, and the desperate desire to possess in retrospect. On the other hand, the poem also is precisely about youth. Youth itself (the condition of being entirely, sensuously in the moment) *is* what the speaker was looking for all through his youth, and misses, and invents, in later years.

But the poem is even more than this. One assumes there may be a confessional element to this poem—Merwin may be reflecting on past loves. But the poem also is clearly allegorical, applicable generally to the situations of many. And certainly, as the poem's last line—"from what we cannot hold the stars are made"—makes clear, the poem's narrative is applicable to many of the key participants in the sonnet tradition. "Youth" thus also turns out to be a fifteen-line sonnet about the psychological, erotic, and elegiac dynamics behind so many sonnets: behind Petrarch's singing to Laura, and Wyatt's imitations of these songs, sung again for his own loves, and

Dante's singing of Beatrice. With "Youth," Merwin has composed an impressive meta-sonnet, a sonnet about sonnets, and in this way puts himself in conversation with some of the poets he greatly values.[24]

Merwin writes:

> [T]here is an affinity which everyone must have noticed between poetry—certain kinds and moments of it—on the one hand, and such succinct forms as the proverb, the aphorism, the riddle, on the other. . . . There are qualities that they obviously have in common: an urge to finality of utterance, for example, and to be irreducible and unchangeable. The urge to brevity is not perhaps as typical of poetry as we would sometimes wish, but the urge to be self-contained, to be whole, is perhaps another form of the same thing, or can be, and it is related to the irreversibility in the words that is the mark of poetry.[25]

In "Youth," which presents a suspenseful riddle that ends in proverblike aphorism, one can see these connections clearly. Certainly, "Youth" is a self-contained poem. But it is not entirely so. And it is the poem's last line—its biggest turn—that does the most to open up the poem. With a suddenness reminiscent of Rilke's "You must change your life" or Wright's "I have wasted my life," Merwin's last line does not contain or close his poem so much as radically expand it, amplifying its meaning and allusive resonance.

A similar dynamic is at play in "The Mole":

> Here is yet one
> more life that we see only from outside
> from the outside
>
> not in itself but later
> in signs of its going
> a reminder
> in the spring daylight
>
> it happened when we were not noticing
> and so close to us
> that we might not have been here
> disregarded as we were

see where we have walked
the earth has risen again
out of its darkness
where it has been recognized
without being seen
known by touch
of the blind velvet fingers
the wise nails
descendants of roots and water

we have seen them
only in death and in pictures
opened from darkness afterward

but here the earth
has been touched and raised
eye has not seen it come
ear has not heard
the famous fur
the moment that finds its way
in the dark without us

In this poem, Merwin presents the mole as an unknown other, "yet one /
more life that we see only from outside." The mole cares nothing for the
humans who might be around it, and the mole's presence is found out only
in retrospect, "in signs of its going," or else "in death and in pictures /
opened from the darkness afterward." The mole, though, ultimately has a
larger significance for Merwin: in the final two lines he equates the mole
with "the moment that finds its way / in the dark without us." At one level
this simply is an excellent turn, shifting from a consideration of the figure
of the mole to a revelation of that figure's meaning—and in doing so it
provides the poem with closure. However, at another level the turn enacts
some of the processes described in the poem, and so opens up the poem
again. Like the mole that is known only in retrospect, the turn itself, an-
other kind of "moment that finds its way / in the dark," sends us back to re-
consider where we have been—we reexamine the terrain after having been
taken by surprise. And suddenly, what were hints leading to a moment are
now traces of that moment, now past. Thus, the major turn in "The Mole"

further activates the poem, asking readers to reread and reconsider their experience of it.

Poems such as "Youth," "The Mole," and "One of the Butterflies" reveal Merwin to be a master of the conceit, of the extended metaphor that his turns often explode or implode. But such poetry is not new to Merwin. Many of his early poems based on myths are, in effect, conceits in which the myth serves as a vehicle for meanings or purposes other than those the myth was likely first designed to convey. In fact, the metaphorical thinking in "The Mole" largely parallels the thinking in "The Moles" from Merwin's 1970 book of prose fables, *The Miner's Pale Children*.[26] There are additional conceits in some of his recent work, including a number of poems featuring extended metaphors in *Present Company* (2005).[27] But in *The Shadow of Sirius* it becomes clear that Merwin, whose first published poem is called "On John Donne," often approaches the status of metaphysical poet.[28]

Perhaps in part inspired by John Donne's own nocturne, "A Nocturnal upon St. Lucy's Day, Being the Shortest Day," Merwin includes two nocturnes in *The Shadow of Sirius*. The first, I think, is particularly elegant and chilling:

Nocturne

The stars emerge one
by one into the names
that were last found for them
far back in other
darkness no one remembers
by watchers whose own
names were forgotten
later in the dark
and as the night deepens
other lumens begin
to appear around them
as though they were shining
through the same instant
from a single depth of age
though the time between
each one of them
and its nearest neighbor
may include in its span

the whole moment of the earth
turning in a light
that is not its own
with the complete course
of life upon it
born to brief reflection
recognition and anguish
from one cell evolving
to remember daylight
laughter and distant music

"Nocturne" is a brilliant and troubling meditation on the night sky. At first the stars come out, taking shape in the constellations assigned to them ages ago. As "the night deepens," so does the meditation. Instead of seeing order-granting constellations, the speaker considers the illusion the night sky creates. While we may think the stars "were shining / through that same instant / from a single depth of age," the fact is that "the time between / each one of them / and its nearest neighbor / contains in its span / the whole moment of the earth / turning in a light / that is not its own." This is a dizzying realization: that the time it takes for light to travel the distance between seemingly close stars actually requires the eons it took for Earth to give birth to life and evolve conscious creatures, including the speaker. In this conceptualization, Earth is a mote swirling around the sun, and the speaker even less.

"Nocturne" turns to acknowledge how life has been "born to brief reflection / recognition and anguish / from one cell evolving / to remember daylight / laughter and distant music." This is a stunning ending. Once again, Merwin's use of rather abstract language is powerful, providing the means to talk simultaneously about all of evolution and a single human life. This is a terrifying temporal collapsing, one that seems permissible due to the temporal confusion from earlier in the poem, and one that seems to have felt the effect of the poem's initial meditation. It is even scarier to be reminded in the poem's last two lines of the music of the spheres, the ancient belief in harmonious, universal, ordering principles. Such consolations are no longer available to us.

In her essay on Merwin, Marjorie Perloff notes that Turner Cassity calls him "a very talented practitioner in a very tired tradition."[29] I hope that some of my comments on Merwin and the surprising turn have served to argue against this perspective, and to argue instead that Merwin is a very talented practitioner of a continuously vital and crucial tradition in poetry.

II / Mark Halliday

So copiously doth my mind o'erbrim with skepticism about Merwin's poetry that too many targets offer themselves at once and I've had trouble deciding where to start in response to Michael Theune's respectful and resourceful interpretation of poems in *Sitting Ducks*. Wait, sorry, the book's title is *The Shadow of Sirius*. But consider this poem, "Your Cloud Returns":

> On the day of your birth
> a bird flew into a cloud
> you heard its song from a place
> between your ears
> the nights came with cold winds
> to carry the cloud far
> above the valleys where dreams turn
> into turnips
> still you wait for that cloud
> to return like a pigeon
> on silent wings of light
> through wave upon wave of wind
> to its home between your ears
> and a day when the song
> becomes your missing name till then
> dream dreamer you are no turnip

What saves this poem from excessively resembling hundreds of poems Merwin has published is the unexpected word "turnip," which violates the patented Merwinesque blue-menthol mood and allows us to remember, for a moment, that visionary romantic aspiration emanates from human creatures with bodies, dietary needs, and pragmatic concerns about book royalties. Unfortunately I can't give Merwin credit for the turnip surprise, because I composed "Your Cloud Returns" in under ten minutes, a way of venting the satirical pressure that built up in me each time I read a few pages of *The Shadow of Sirius*.

Substitute "raindrop" for "turnip" in "Your Cloud Returns" and then let's ask a Merwin aficionado to explain why my poem is not as pleasing as countless Merwin poems. I don't think a convincing case could be made against "Your Cloud Returns" that wouldn't also pop the small blue balloons of most poems in *Shadow* and indeed in many other Merwin books, all the way back to *The Moving Target* (1963). Reading Merwin, either you've got faith or you've got unbelief—that is, he asks for an entirely credulous reader, a reader who endlessly feels that poetry can carry us very efficiently to a condition of transcendent awareness of Essential Being. For such a reader, skepticism is not even in the ballgame. (And "ballgame" is a vulgarly inappropriate metaphor for the séancelike experience that Merwin offers.) A devoted Merwin reader is marvelously ready to be lifted away from the level of quotidian irritation, competition, sexual desire, economic need, envy, humor, cars, movies, blogs, and turnips, up to the level of safely unspecific archetypes. Merwin should release a CD in which he dispenses with verbs and syntax altogether and simply utters—with calm wistfulness—strings of nouns: bird sky mountain light lake silence sleep darkness cloud trees earth river dream stars. . . . There would be buyers.

Well, that sort of sardonic remark about Merwin's vocabulary has been made by numerous critics, without shaking what Michael Theune calls (in a phrase more devastating than he himself acknowledges) Merwin's "systematic confidence." After all, only a poet utterly impervious to satire and utterly deaf to irony would call his book of short philosophical musings (extremely reminiscent of his innumerable previous musings) *The Shadow of Sirius*. Why not call it *The Odor of Really Not Kidding?* Merwin's persistence in being Merwinesque is not at all surprising. He developed a prizewinning manner five decades ago, and he's no Yeats capable of finding new voices in himself. Besides, as Theune has crucially observed (in another phrase far more damagingly apt than the critic himself admits), "Merwin—we can see it plainly now—is a poet of great equilibrium and poise." Merwin is not about the painful exploration of tensions, fears, desires, failures, conflicts, confusions. Indeed, he is never for more than a flickering moment even about the *exploration* (as distinct from the declaration) of loss and sorrow. The unguent of his narcotically languid style is always there to embalm and ostensibly heal the cuts and bruises inflicted by time.

No deep surprises are to be expected from Merwin. What does surprise me is that a critic as astute as Theune can talk himself into calling him "a craftsman of surprise." Theune is fascinated by the phenomenon of *the turn* in poems, and his criticism centered on this idea has seemed to me, in other contexts, extraordinarily useful. But in the case of Merwin I will argue that Theune's readiness to find a *turn* (where I seldom see more than a mild and well-oiled shifting of gears) has made him far too generous, far too willing to say that a mere ripple—as when an old man's nostalgia slides into an old man's wishfulness or faint transcendental hope or sighing resignation—is a surprise.

Let's keep in mind that it's one thing for a person to say he is surprised (amazed, astonished, ga-ga with wonder) and another thing for him to *be* surprised. And it is yet *another* thing for a person (whether truly surprised or not) to surprise us in his poem.

To make my case against *The Shadow of Sirius* I could gather some of the most obviously static and banal poems and focus on them, but I hope it will be more interesting to focus on the poems that Theune has singled out.

"The Mole" is a poem about the strange otherness of an animal. As such it can be listed in a tradition that includes many good poems by D. H. Lawrence (notably "Snake") and Rilke's "The Panther" and Robinson Jeffers's "Hurt Hawks" and Marianne Moore's "The Pangolin" and Randall Jarrell's "Bats" and "The Chipmunk's Day" and Ted Hughes's "Hawk Roosting" and George MacBeth's "Owl" and Mary Jo Salter's "Kangaroo." To say, though, that Merwin's poem is in conversation with that tradition would be to give credit where credit is not due; "The Mole" barely amounts to an enervated nod to that tradition. Where does Merwin convincingly or interestingly imagine the mole's experience? Is it where he writes that the mole knows the earth "by touch / of the blind velvet fingers / the wise nails / descendants of roots and water"? This writing is so flimsy. To refer to a mole's claws as fingers is lazily anthropomorphic; to call them blind because the mole's eyes are nearly blind is at best loosely metonymic; to associate the mole's paws with velvet seems more sentimental than perceptive. What about saying that the mole's nails are wise? I might be able to approve of the phrase in a poem that registered awareness of its silliness. If you're not amused by the wise nails of Merwin's mole, you deserve to read many poems about the raccoon's meditative gaze and the clever tail of the beaver. Is it brilliant of Merwin to remark that the mole's wise nails are "descendants of roots and water"? They are also descendants of carbon and oxygen, but it would be less lyrical to say so. Is there any part of any animal's body that is not a descendant of roots and water, when you get right down to it? If any are, surely all are. I like Thomas Hardy's "Proud Songsters," which ends with the awed acknowledgment that a year ago the young birds "No finches were, nor nightingales, / Nor thrushes, / But only particles of grain, / And earth, and air, and rain." To justify my preference for Hardy's poem over Merwin's might require a page of arguing but would depend on my sense that Hardy's awe is deeply felt while Merwin's remark about "roots and water" seems casual, phoned-in.

However, Theune's praise for "The Mole" doesn't worry about whether Merwin has intensely imagined his animal, nor about his embarrassingly obvious emphasis on the fact that we can't see the mole as it travels underground. Instead Theune finds so much metaphorical significance in the poem's penultimate line, which substitutes "moment" for "mole," that Merwin is revealed as "a master of the conceit" and indeed almost a metaphysical poet. The mole has done its thing without people having perceived its activity; here are the poem's last four lines:

> ear has not heard
> the famous fur
> the moment that finds its way
> in the dark without us

(I realize that funniness indexes personality, and that you can't prove something is funny; but for me, the lines "ear has not heard / the famous fur" are either a terrific instance of inadvertent funniness or an extremely rare indication that Merwin does have a sense of humor.) I agree that if "The Mole" has a chance to be an interesting poem, it depends overwhelmingly on the word "moment." Theune judges the last two lines to be not only "an excellent turn" but a revelation that the whole poem has not essentially been about the furry underground animal, but rather about a mental experience in which we belatedly realize that a hidden process has followed its course—we see its result only when the process has ended.

That theme *can* be poignant—as many poems by Hardy demonstrate—but I don't think it is poignant in "The Mole." Its delivery is so brief, so professionally efficient. Merwin sensed that the poem needed some metaphorical flicker (something a turn-seeker could conceivably call a turn) and he supplied it with one word. Why is "moment" the right word there? Why not "dream" or "belief" or "longing" or "hunger" or "desire" or "knowing" or "search" or "hope" or "revelation"? Any of these words might have given Theune a more coherent turn than "moment." More coherent, I say, though not wondrous or surprising. But after all, if "moment" does deliver a tiny surprise, does it also bring insight? The mole has worked in the ground for hours (hunting insects and worms)—how is the mole like a *moment?* Well, its invisible existence consisted of a series of moments: dig, dig, dig, eat. Got it! The insight Theune celebrates, though, concerns our experience as readers: when we reach the end of the poem "suddenly, what were hints leading to a moment are now traces of that moment, now past." (Notice that this account doesn't evoke the actual mole's experience—its digging and digging was hard work, not a series of mysterious hints pointing toward some as-yet-unknown future condition.) I'm afraid that as a description of a reader's experience, Theune's remark either dissolves into a useless mindbender (the early parts of a poem lead us toward what we feel when we arrive at the end of the poem and then when we look back at them we realize they were setting up that feeling which is now already a remembered feeling) or turns out to describe the reading of *any* poem.

So I think Theune's interest in the end of "The Mole" is a case of something often seen: a smart critic working too hard on behalf of a poet who hasn't worked hard enough. Another example: Merwin's extremely simple "Nocturne" can't bear the weight of praise Theune pours upon it. Paraphrased, "Nocturne" says that the stars in the night sky were named long ago by people whose own names have been forgotten, and that when other stars appear they seem to resemble the first-seen stars, whereas actually some of them are vastly older than others—Merwin spends some fifteen lines establishing this astronomical nugget and still doesn't say it very clearly—"the time between / each one of them / and its nearest neighbor / contains in its span / the whole moment of the earth. . . ." You could be forgiven for inferring that he means something about *distance* between stars. If it weren't for the Holy Hush that Merwin promotes via short lines and chaste abstention from punctuation, the pedestrian prosaic quality of his (oddly confusing) astronomy factoid would be far more apparent. (The age and size of the cosmos are undoubtedly stupendous. Carl Sagan or any of his colleagues can impress us with this. But a poem is meant to give us something fresher, stranger, and deeper than a planetarium mini-lecture.) If Theune finds it chilling, I think he must be reacting not to any special achievement of Merwin's language but simply to his own astonishment at the immensity of space.

Next, in the final five lines of "Nocturne," Merwin describes life on earth as

> born to brief reflection
> recognition and anguish
> from one cell evolving
> to remember daylight
> laughter and distant music

Is this a stunning ending, as Theune says? He's right that Merwin's hazy syntax allows the lines to refer simultaneously to a single human life and all lives ever lived on earth. The ambiguity is skillful, if you like (though to me it seems slippery the way poor prose is often slippery), but what interesting thought about one human life or all human life is presented here? No interesting thought at all! We are simply asked to be moved by a generalizing summary in which six nouns *(reflection, recognition, anguish, daylight, laughter, music)* remind us that here on earth there has been a whole lotta shakin' goin' on. (How desperately a Merwin book makes me thankful for Jerry Lee Lewis!) Merwin is enough of a pro to know that a reference to music (song, singing) in the last line of a poem ensures what the average reader feels is poeticality. I feel the tug, but I resist it here because the move is so naked, so threadbare.

With the skill of an adept critic Theune evokes "a terrifying temporal collapsing" in Merwin's simultaneous reference to one lifetime and all terrestrial life. But we've heard before that the long story of life on earth is like an eyeblink in the duration of the cosmos. I don't see that Merwin has managed to render this truth freshly frightening. Theune is adroit when he hears in the final phrase of "Nocturne"—"distant music"—an allusion to the medieval faith in the music of the spheres; probably if I saw real value elsewhere in the poem, I'd be glad to accept this allusion as an added felicity—as a turn, even.

But "Nocturne" is far too anemic to be mentioned in the same sentence with Donne's "A Nocturnal upon St. Lucy's Day, Being the Shortest Day." Intrinsic to the vast superiority of Donne's midnight poem is the way Donne makes us feel his presence—as a particular individual on a certain night, a man so frozen in grief that he feels worthless. "I, by love's limbeck, am the grave / of all that's nothing"—Donne's self-condemnation is so convincingly felt that it cuts through to the place in one's own spirit where one has felt worthless. There is nothing even remotely personal revealed in Merwin's "Nocturne"—nor in "Nocturne II," which ends with these harmlessly nice lines: ". . . I lie in the dark / listening to what I remember / while the night flies on with us into itself". What *do* you remember, sir? The mood of *Shadow* may be mainly elegiac, but if so it is remarkable how scattered and unspecific or impersonally generic are Merwin's references to his past.

(There are a few fortunate exceptions to this. Hurrah for Billy Green, who "explained to me about sex" in "Child Light," and hurrah for the 1922 Webster's Dictionary that prompts Merwin to write a few specific lines about his father in "Inheritance"—not strong poems, these, but still touchingly elegiac.)

The general absence of personal details in *Shadow* is an aspect of its pervasive impersonality, which the Donne comparison calls to mind. Donne's "Nocturnal" dwells in and explores spiritual pain. Certainly there is a sense in which Donne attains (we feel) equilibrium and poise through the art of his poem; this is, thank goodness, essential to what art can do. But in Donne the equilibrium and poise are reached by way of an intense (while artfully mediated) confrontation with pain—pain that remains undissolved at poem's end. Merwin's poetic project, in contrast, is a shortcut to equilibrium; he is always fast-forwarding past any painful facts to the floaty calm of white space. Merwin's poetry is constantly self-medicating. (It's as if a whole book, and most of a long career, were devoted to the comfort-seeking mood that takes control of Wallace Stevens's "World Without Peculiarity.") Any painful reality of past or present must immediately be tamed, shrouded in a Holy Hush, so as to preserve what Theune calls Merwin's late-style "super-serene."

And I won't forbear to suggest more specifically that the Merwin serenity has a savor of self-esteem. Again, it is the juxtaposition with Donne's "Nocturnal" that brings this into focus. Where does Merwin ever seriously question the moral soundness or the spiritual integrity of a particular choice he has made or condition into which he has fallen? When does he need what Hopkins needs when he writes "I wake and feel the fell of dark, not day" or "My own heart let me more have pity on"? One pervasive subtext of *The Shadow of Sirius* is: Being so old is worrisome, but still it's nice to be Merwin.

To Merwin's admirers that remark will seem perverse, since the book is filled with instances of yearning. My argument (again) is that Merwin keeps registering his yearning rather than exploring it. As the pages pass there is to my mind a cumulative effect of programmatic yearning by a Professional Yearner content to produce a publishable puff of yearning between cups of coffee. Does Merwin ever look at a draft and think "That's banal!"? Let's remember that yearning is fundamental to the work of *any* serious poet; a poem arises in response to something unsatisfying or disappointing in reality—such as the inevitability of loss. Therefore a poet who directly declares his yearning is doing less subtly what all serious poets do. Now, direct statement of feeling or theme *can* be powerful in poetry—"It is Margaret you mourn for"—when juxtaposed with other elements. What bothers me is that Merwin (like his fans) seems to feel that yearning *in itself* makes him special.

I said I wouldn't target the most vulnerable poems in *Shadow*—but here is one egregious example of the Half A Muffin poem (you wouldn't have time to eat the whole muffin before you finished writing the poem), "My Hand":

> See how the past is not finished
> here in the present
> it is awake the whole time
> never waiting
> it is my hand now but not what I held
> it is not my hand but what I held

it is what I remember
but it never seems quite the same
no one else remembers it
a house long gone into air
the flutter of tires over a brick road
cool light in a vanished bedroom
the flash of the oriole
between one life and another
the river a child watched

That poem so needs some lines about kissing a girl named Marcia under the streetlight at the corner of Wade and Dogwood while gnats swarmed overhead. Marcia's long dark hair. Marcia's bicycle, her fingers on the handlebars. But even Marcia probably couldn't save "My Hand" from its helpless goshness. Imagine being an unfamous poet trying to publish this poem.

"Youth" is one of the most abstract poems in *Shadow* and one of the most direct in expression of yearning. In a way these qualities make the poem impressive, since it confidently abjures even the wispiest autobiographical gesture. Theune writes well about how the object of Merwin's lifelong search can be understood either as a beloved person (perhaps a wife, or an ideal amalgam of many loved women?) or as youth itself. Or both. Theune calls "Youth" a fifteen-line "meta-sonnet" about the haunted centrality of desire that animates the long tradition of sonnets. That sounds right, and the poem does have a certain classic air; I'm not quite willing to call it a bad poem. However, I squint at its tacked-on fifteenth line: "from what we cannot hold the stars are made"—here Merwin goes for the three-point swish from way downtown. Nothing but net? Theune says the line radically expands the poem, but I feel the line is a leap into blarney. Are the stars made of longing for transcendent union with the beloved? Or are they made of burning gases? Well, we cannot hold burning gases. True! And your desire for your beloved, is it essentially a chemical explosion? Maybe! I think the line "from what we cannot hold the stars are made" is skillfully packaged to cause an audience to gasp. It is consciously quotable. But it is not evidently thoughtful. If it is a turn, it is not a good turn.

Theune mentions another poem of yearning, "One of the Butterflies," as evidence that Merwin is "a master of the conceit"—but it actually presents only the flipside of a conceit, in that the only metaphorical image in the poem is in its title; the body of the poem is abstract generalization about the ephemerality of pleasure. I'll quote the whole poem and ask the reader to consider whether it offers any thought about pleasure that is, on a moment's reflection, even faintly unfamiliar.

One of the Butterflies

The trouble with pleasure is the timing
it can overtake me without warning
and be gone before I know it is here
it can stand facing me unrecognized
while I am remembering somewhere else
in another age or someone not seen
for years and never to be seen again
in this world and it seems that I cherish
only now a joy I was not aware of
when it was here although it remains
out of reach and will not be caught or named
or called back and if I could make it stay
as I want to it would turn into pain

"One of the Butterflies" is a blatant case of an idea for a poem substituting for an unwritten poem. You could say it is different from midcareer Merwin because it lacks archetypal Nature Legos (river trees wind bird rain smoke light stars), but what a limp version of late-career change. Imagine what the author of "Ode on Melancholy" would think of Merwin's colorless ephemerid.

The thought of Keats prompts the recognition that Merwin is much more Shelleyan than Keatsian—that is, Merwin is strongly inclined to aim straight toward Essential Truths, and when he employs images en route, the images tend to be abstracted and generic (ever since *The Moving Target*). If Shelley is a far greater poet than Merwin, as I suppose, it's largely because Merwin can't match Shelley's philosophical originality and ambition. As for Keats's wonderful bringing-to-life of the rich relations between physical and psychological experiences, Merwin isn't even in the ring.

Reader, I am sixty-two. Already I can feel in my limbs how old age will be no picnic. Seeing young women on the street, I feel the vanishing of possibility. Every day I stare into space wondering, where did the time go? Everything glowed with a gleam, but it's as if I must have been look-ing away. So I'm not unsympathetic to the themes that mesmerize Merwin in *The Shadow of Sirius*; I too try to write elegiac and time-dazed poems. I try, though, to give the poems not just white bones but flesh and blood. To do so involves giving a sense of an unpretentious real speaker who speaks from his entanglement in life, struggling to get something across to a lis-tener who may have different perceptions. We may say that a poem strives ultimately to reach an apprehension that is beyond language—to evoke the unsayable; this is perhaps true (though we could invite professional philosophers to debate where and when the notion of an apprehension beyond language has meaning) but can become an excuse for poems that too smoothly bypass the complexities of expression that make poetry (for poetry people) more interesting than philosophy.

During the Vietnam War public discourse was felt by many Americans to be so horribly corrupted that a longing arose for words that would escape conventional utterance and Break On Through to essential truth. Merwin was ahead of the curve on this—by 1963 he was already developing a style marvelously suited to that longing. The two keys are total absence of punc-tuation and constant recourse to archetypal nouns (adorned with very few adjectives). When I graduated from college in 1971, my friends and I were enthralled with Merwin.

I like to think, though, that by the time of *The Carrier of Ladders* in 1970 I had already sensed that something too simple might be going on. I do remember that when *Writings to an Unfinished Accompaniment* appeared in 1973, I felt a wave of revulsion—that book's title in itself, at once so clunky and so preening, seemed a signal that I would need to find poetry very different from this drifto-smoothie poetry. And it also woke me up to the fact that fame begets more fame, because most readers (and publishers!) of poetry want to be assured that a poet is big and important rather than alarmingly unfamous. And here we are in 2011, writing about Merwin.

Merwin is not without talent. If the dozen best poems in *Shadow* were mixed in with quite different poems (about complicated disturbing feel-ings in complicated specific experiences), they would no doubt look better to me. In such a collection I'd be more open to the evocation of his par-ents' experience of existential bafflement in "Secrets," and to the pathos—

simple, ordinary, but affectingly vivid—of that poem's closing lines about his mother's death:

> and was the veil still there
> when my mother turned from her own garden one evening that same year
>
> telling a friend on the telephone that she was going
> to get some rest now and her glasses were lying
>
> apart from her on the floor not more than an hour
> later when a neighbor pushed the door open and found her

And I'd be more accepting of "Shadow Hand," a decent sweet elegy for a roofer named Duporte whose worldly wisdom impressed Merwin when he was a boy. No poem could be more conventional, but it is impossible to dislike, and it ends with vivid lines prompted by Merwin's long-belated discovery that Duporte has died:

> it seemed as though it had just
> happened and it had not been long
> since we stood in the road talking
> about owls nesting in chimneys
> in the dark in empty houses

If Theune wants to call that a turn, I won't argue, though I'd be more likely to call it a surprisingly apt metaphorical illustration. Another poem impossible to dislike (well, I can imagine a coldhearted Young Turk making fun of it, but still) is "The Pinnacle," in which Merwin remembers a retired teacher, Miss Giles, who went for a walk with him when he was a little boy. The poem's sweetness is so genuine, so unmannered, that for me this poem is the pinnacle of *The Shadow of Sirius*. It captures the wonderstruck child who has, I think, persisted in Merwin's work under several disguises for some fifty years, an aspect of personality hard to distinguish from the poet's impulse toward the radical simplicity of timeless archetypes. Wonderstruck children are nice, and super-serene old folks are also nice; but great poetry is written by anxious ambivalent strenuous adults.

III / Michael Theune

". . . turn / into turnips." *Turnips*! Brilliant!

However, while "Your Cloud Returns" is a wonderful parody by an excellent poet and critic, I think the poem's status as parody reveals itself a bit earlier than Mark Halliday indicates: the reveal occurs in "from a place / between your ears." In those lines, Halliday makes the mind material by situating it bodily, and Merwin is not apt to do this. For all the mental activities—the recognition, the memory, the grieving, the wondering—that occur in Merwin's poems, one rarely, if ever, encounters an axon or a dendrite, let alone Psyche's "soft-conched ear."

While Merwin's imagination, like every artist's, has its limits, I think those limits have served him well. He has gone deep into the territory he has staked out, to become an astute phenomenologist of the imagining mind, a poet who makes the workings of the mind palpable.

One can see this kind of work occurring in "My Hand." "My Hand" is a fairly sophisticated poem about some of the ways "the past"—that convenient name we give to an active, amorphous mass of memory and information—is "not finished" for the remembering mind. To remember well, the remembering mind must allow some objects to come into focus and let others recede. This shiftiness is captured in the lines "it is my hand now but not what I held / it is not my hand but what I held." The past also changes depending on present circumstances, including the conditions of remembrance, and even including the existence of others who might remember the same incidents—I likely will remember an incident differently if I am aware that I am the last one who remembers it. This is what Merwin is getting at when he states, "it is what I remember / but it never seems quite the same / no one else remembers it."

The rest of the poem offers glimpses of such shifted memories, including a house one remembers that is now, in fact, "long gone," and, almost simultaneously, tries to account for how those constantly transforming memories *seem*, how they *feel*. This second part of the poem is not perfect—"the flash of the oriole / between one life and another" feels a bit forced—but parts of it are, I think, deeply resonant. For example, "the flutter of tires over a brick road" offers a truly complex image, an emblem of memory, of the contemporary (the fast-moving tires) both meeting and not meeting the past (the brick road). An amazing act of synesthesia (the sound effect arises from what in fact is a visual image) makes that image, that idea, palpable, makes it memorable, places it (paradoxically) solidly between my ears.

The poem's final line, "the river a child watched," also feels properly insistent to me. It is strangely shocking to install a child by the river, eternal symbol of the flow of time, into which (supposedly) one cannot step twice—the effect is uncanny. The last lines of Merwin's "No Shadow" are "the river still seems not to move / as though it were the same river," but I think it would be wrong to understand the end of "My Hand" as merely saying the same thing. Paul Celan notes that "'[a]ll things are aflowing': this thought included—and does that not bring everything to a halt?"[30] A reverie upon oneself when one was likely in reverie—watching a river flow—not only constitutes a statement about impermanence but also demands that readers perform a mental action similar to the one captured in Celan's aphorism. There's a halting progression, a stutter step, in the last line of "My Hand," in which the flow of time, the past, is folded or knotted and our sense of the past is altered, perhaps deepened. It may in fact be that "the past is not finished / here in the present."

In some respects, Halliday is correct about "My Hand": it does not contain examples of the randomness of memory, nor of the tendency of memory to replay erotically charged moments. "My Hand" certainly is a tightly controlled poem: it has an idea, extends that idea, and then offers evidence for the idea. But it is a good poem, I think, somewhat better than Halliday thinks it is. It may be half a muffin, but it's the top half.

However, it is not "My Hand" but rather one of Merwin's dog elegies that is one of the great poems in *The Shadow of Sirius* of making the imagining mind palpable:

Dream of Koa Returning

Sitting on the steps of that cabin
that I had always known
with its porch and gray-painted floorboards
I looked out to the river
flowing beyond the big trees
and all at once you
were just behind me

lying watching me
as you did years ago
and not stirring at all
when I reached back slowly
hoping to touch
your long amber fur
and there we stayed without moving
listening to the river
and I wondered whether
it might be a dream
whether you might be a dream
whether we both were a dream
in which neither of us moved

On one level, "Dream of Koa Returning" recalls the movement of an imagin-
ing, remembering mind: the speaker recalls a strong memory of being with
the dog ("all at once you / were just behind me"), a recollection that makes
him meditate on the reality of his present situation. Nothing terribly pro-
found in this—we all know the story of how Chuang Tzu had such a strong
dream about being a butterfly that when he awakened he did not know if
he was a philosopher dreaming he was a butterfly or a butterfly dreaming
he was a philosopher. But "Dream of Koa Returning" is more complex than
this. Due to the strategic deployment of abstraction, Merwin creates a great
deal of temporal play and overlapping in this poem. For example, when the
speaker reacts bodily to the presence of the dog, "reach[ing] back slowly /
hoping to touch / [its] long amber fur," one cannot tell if this is taking place
in the distant past or in the simple past of the poem, or both. Merwin cre-
ates a space of ghostly simultaneity.

But the true power of this poem arrives with its last two lines. Try to
imagine the poem without them: it remains little more than a retelling of
Chuang Tzu's parable. The problem with Chuang Tzu's parable is that after
hearing it no one actually believes, or feels, that she or he really is a dream-
ing butterfly—life is simply not so deeply mysterious. In a mere retelling
such a possibility is only indicated, not evoked. But with the last two lines
of "Dream of Koa Returning," Merwin turns narration into evocation. The
penultimate line takes dreaming away from the poem's speaker and dog,
and as a result, the dream could be anything's, or anyone's, including the

reader's. But so far this is an easy trick, the simplicity of which one can sense by imagining the poem ending "in the mind of the reader." The genius of "Dream of Koa Returning" occurs in its last line, where suddenly the reader is granted a strong sense of the way the acts of physically turning and reaching make mental images come alive—a sense made stronger by means of erasure. (Though it's paradoxical, anyone startled by the death of Wordsworth's boy of Winander knows how powerful images can be *especially* when they are taken away.) That is, instructed to think so, the reader imagined something turned, but then is reminded that no such turning took place—after all, this was all in the reader's imagination; nothing *actually* turned. But the imagining, especially at its moment of loss, *did* seem real. In "Dream of Koa Returning," Merwin shows readers that their minds are capable of truly wondrous feats, of making deeply mysterious dreams that *feel* palpable and real, dreams in which it seems the impossible can take place.

Merwin has been thinking about such melding for some time. In an undergraduate essay on Alexander Pope, he wrote, "There is an affinity in [Pope's] style to those Chinese poets who build complete poems in seventeen syllables. The formal balance of one couplet against another, and of phrase against phrase within couplet line, of proposition in line #1 and resolution in line #2 may not be the highest of virtues but it is a virtue."[31] Like Merwin's "worn words," this idea has "been there" for him, though he himself has come far from thinking that all the second element in a haiku or couplet can do is resolve what came before it—he knows, and shows, that the relationship between poetic parts is much more complex than this, that the second element can, for example, deepen, question, negate, illuminate, even *activate* what came before it. And in the process Merwin has done his part to raise the skillful, surprising transition between one part of a poem and another to a very high virtue indeed.

"The Mole" yokes together such disparate poetic approaches and concerns, and even after considering Halliday's insightful critiques, I remain intrigued by the poem's turn. "The Mole" is not, as Halliday states, "a poem about the strange otherness of an animal." Rather, it is about the strange otherness of the moment. In this way, "The Mole" behaves like the emblem poems it so closely resembles: Oliver Wendell Holmes's "The Chambered

Nautilus," Robert Frost's "Design," and Jorie Graham's "Prayer." Emblem poems are not so much about the ostensible otherness of the creature(s) they incorporate, be it a chambered nautilus, a moth and a spider, or a school of minnows. Instead, emblem poems primarily are about what those creatures represent, whether a message from heaven, an argument against design, or our powerlessness against forces much greater than us.

Merwin employs the mole in his emblem poem—a poetic mode deeply connected to aspects of Christian theology—to think about the mystical moment more central to particular strands of Buddhist thought. His point is to reveal that the moment, so prized as an end of human endeavor, so sought after, is itself an impersonal force, unconcerned with human well-being, that gets along just fine "without us." But why does the mole represent specifically "the moment"? Oddly enough, I think the answer to this question lies less in the nature of the mole and more in the situation of the speaker and his companion(s). "[N]ot noticing" what is really going on around them, the speaker and his companion(s) seem to be much more interested "in the spring daylight." They seem to be in search of a rather clichéd "moment" where they expect to find it: on an idyllic outing. Or perhaps prior to seeing the traces of the mole they thought they in fact *were* in the moment. Either way, one needs to read and understand what Merwin writes simply as "the moment" containing within it "The Moment." And *that* moment in the poem is shocking, surprising, ironic, even funny—so much so that it sends one (it sent me) back to reconsider the poem, the dynamics—yes, to be sure—of reading any *good* poem.

One last poem from me:

Falling

Long before daybreak
none of the birds yet awake
rain comes down with the sound
of a huge wind rushing
through the valley trees
it comes down around us
all at the same time
and beyond it there is nothing
it falls without hearing itself

without knowing
there is anyone here
without seeing where it is
or where it is going
like a moment of great
happiness of our own
that we cannot remember
coasting with the lights off

In "A Letter to Su Tung-p'o," Merwin writes, "Almost a thousand years later / I am asking the same questions." "Falling" is one of the poems in which Merwin proves this claim true. In "Hsin-ch'ou Eleventh Month, Nineteenth Day," Su Tung-p'o asks his brother, "When will we listen to the soft rustle of night rain?"[32] In Merwin's poem the question is similar, but the treatment is different. Unlike Su Tung-p'o's wonderful, rangey poem, Merwin writes a poem, wonderful as well, focused almost wholly on the night rain, listening to it, wondering about it, meditating on it. I find the description of the rain shockingly evocative. Though abstract, the description works, and it may work in large part because it is abstract, like a strange wash of static. I hear the rain's rushing crescendo. The middle part of the poem is the kind of meditation that one is familiar with in Merwin's poems: the rain is not there for the one considering it; the rain has no purpose. (I of course know this, in the same way that I know that the stars are very far apart, but I also keep forgetting that I know it and need reminding. Merwin reminds me.)

Then, in its last four lines, the poem turns, delivering surprise after surprise. "[L]ike a moment of great . . . *happiness*"? That seems marvelously simultaneously wrong (according to the pathetic fallacy) and right (like Merwin, and Su Tung-p'o, and many others, I love storms). But that happiness is suddenly strangely qualified: "happiness of our own / that we cannot remember." What a wild paradox, a lovely idea! And this, it seems to me, is the heart of the poem; the effort of this poem largely seems to be to convince readers of the existence of this strange mental state, this joy that can't ever be accurately recalled but must, and can, be evoked, conjured up, for us. However, at this point in the poem this notion is merely asserted, and the poem is only a mediocre nature poem. The reader must still be convinced that there is a category of experience that might be called "happiness of our own / that we cannot remember." Such confirmation comes in the last line: "coasting with the lights off". Here is another example of a thrilling happiness we can feel in only the strangest of ways, that we can own but, because so much of it occurs mysteriously and in darkness, we cannot fully remember.

"Falling," like so many Merwin poems, is a poem of wit, which occurs, as Barbara Herrnstein Smith notes, "when expectations are simultaneously surprised and fulfilled."[33] Only the masters, such as John Donne and Bashō, have command over it. But Merwin does, as well, and in a rather unusual way. In *Lyric Powers,* Robert von Hallberg distinguishes between "orphic" and "rhetorical" poets.[34] Merwin is a hybrid of these two types, skillfully deploying rhetorical strategies to achieve orphic ends. He has equilibrium and poise, but I want to be clear: he's got the equilibrium and poise of a great sorcerer who needs only to make a few gestures to cast a strong enchantment, to use a few words to make superb, highly charged lyrical events, to make sparks fly in the thinking and feeling mind.

IV / Mark Halliday

Suppose you wake up at four o'clock in the morning and hear a rainstorm beginning outside. The rain comes on strong, torrential—and you lie there listening. You're fascinated by the way the rain is so fully itself, gives itself so entirely to being what it is. The rain is free from ambivalence. You feel that in this way the rain is profoundly different from you—because nearly all the time you are divided, anxious, ambivalent, paradoxical, self-contradictory. (Rain doesn't need to write poems.) But then why do you somehow feel a kinship with this rainstorm? The rain is not conscious—it has no idea what it is doing—whereas you are (ironically, hopefully, regretfully, wearily, painfully) conscious in all your waking hours. All? No, you feel there must have been moments in your life when you *were* like the rainstorm: wholly given over to sheer being. And you feel that such moments must have been very happy.

Okay—do you have the ingredients for an interesting poem that will evoke these 4:00 a.m. sensations and thoughts? Maybe you do. Maybe you could write a better poem than Merwin's "Falling." I don't think it would be hard to do so, since he presents the subject in such a skeletal way. "Falling" is aimed at a reader so ready for hypnosis that the sorcerer (as Theune calls Merwin) "needs only to make a few gestures to cast a strong enchantment"—whereas a skeptical reader like me begins to smile as Merwin describes the unconscious rainstorm:

> it comes down around us
> all at the same time
> and beyond it there is nothing
> it falls without hearing itself
> without knowing
> there is anyone here
> without seeing where it is
> or where it is going

To hear those lines the way I hear them, imagine them spoken by Christopher Guest's character Nigel Tufnel in *This Is Spinal Tap* or by Eric Idle or by a ponytailed hipster who wants to sell you some incense. Merwin does, after all, offer these lines for sale. It takes a kind of nerve.

Those lines about the rain are so flatly obvious that "Falling" desperately needs an interesting, unexpected ending. Merwin says that the mindless downpour is "like a moment of great / happiness of our own / that we cannot remember"—and I agree, grudgingly, that as an *idea* this is not empty; we may feel that such moments have occurred in our lives, moments when we were happily at one with our activity, without self-consciousness—and that the reason why we can't remember such moments is that during them we had no thought of ourselves. This idea is not startling or strange, but I grant that it is interesting enough as an idea. My point is that the *writing,* in the three lines just quoted, is not interesting. Theune says that Merwin uses "rhetorical strategies to achieve orphic ends." In practice this often means that Merwin attaches nakedly direct and simple *statement* to a flurry of his archetypal props (birds rain wind valley trees) and the juxtaposition, rendered sacramental-ish by nonpunctuation, proposes to be deep. Where is the sorcery? Theune admits that up until the final line "this notion is merely asserted, and the poem is only a mediocre nature poem."

So everything depends on the final line: "coasting with the lights off". Theune feels the unexpectedness of this line lifts "Falling" to the level of mastery. I agree that the line is deftly surprising, a welcome escape from abstractions. However, does the line pass the Cool Second Thought test? What was your vehicle, Mr. Merwin, when you were coasting with the lights off? A car? Bicycle? Speedboat? Was it not dangerous to coast with your lights off? If it was dangerous, is such risky behavior really what you want to compare to the innocent rainstorm? And, if it was dangerous, or mock-dangerous, was it really unselfconscious?

Perhaps Halliday thinks too literally! I realize that many metaphors want to work on us suddenly—"Petals on a wet, black bough"—and that all metaphors break down at some point (subway riders are not entirely like flowers, etc.). But the best metaphors have a buoyant resistance to skepticism, because there is so much rightness in them. I question whether this is true about "coasting with the lights off".

"Dream of Koa Returning" is sweetly sad: Merwin misses his long-dead dog, and for a moment imagines the dog is alive again behind him as he sits watching a river. (Not reading *The New Yorker*, or washing the dishes, no; watching a river, natch.) What coldhearted reader would not be affected by this poem? Possibly any reader familiar with Hardy's great poem "The Shadow on the Stone." After the death of his wife Emma, Hardy walks in their garden and sees cast on a stone a shadow that seems her shadow, as if she were behind him working in the garden. The poem maintains an exquisitely rigorous tension between Hardy's rational knowledge that Emma is dead and his irrational or extrarational sensation of her presence: "and to keep down grief / I would not turn my head to discover / That there was nothing in my belief." Theune says that in the Koa poem Merwin "creates a space of ghostly simultaneity"—whereas I feel Merwin limply gestures toward this; if you want to see the creation of ghostly simultaneity (between disbelieving and believing), read "The Shadow on the Stone."

> So I went on softly from the glade,
> And left her behind me throwing her shade,
> As she were indeed an apparition—
> My head unturned lest my dream should fade.[35]

Now, I realize that to be good, a poem need not be superior to, or equal to, a great poem on the same subject. But for me, Hardy's poem with its much fuller rendering of the experience of wistful illusion (caused by an actual shadow, whereas Merwin's illusion comes out of nowhere) helps expose the limitations of Merwin's poem. Setting aside the comparison, though, is there not an aroma of inadvertent self-parody when Merwin writes:

> and I wondered whether
> it might be a dream
> whether you might be a dream
> whether we both were a dream

—the next line should be "dreamed by a cuckoo sleeping on the roof." But the poem's last line is "in which neither of us moved". Theune adroitly finds ambiguity in the line—maybe Merwin never did reach for Koa!—but no such ambiguity redeems the poem from its air of sleepy passivity which is hard to distinguish from complacency.

Personality is always inseparable from our responses to poems. It is good for us to compare our responses, and try to explain them; to do this makes us less lonely. Sooner or later, though, we reach the place where each reader says to the other, "It just doesn't feel that way to me." As a reader, I tend to feel skeptical about any poem that strikes me as cheaply mysterious. That is, among the many possible objections that a reader can have to a poem, cheapness-of-mystery comes more quickly to my mind than to the minds of some other readers. (For some readers, meanwhile, "prosiness" comes to mind very readily as a high-priority objection, whereas for me this objection tends to be secondary or tertiary.) As I've said, I grew suspicious of Merwin long ago, in the 1970s, after an initial phase of beguilement. My emerging skepticism about Merwin had much to do with my own efforts to write truthful poems. By the time I was thirty, I belatedly realized—helped by my mentor Frank Bidart—that for me the interesting truths of human experience were tangled, awkward, unsleek, and often embarrassing. Has Merwin ever written a poem in which we feel that he himself feels seriously embarrassed? If so, I would tend to prefer that poem to any of his myriad Holy Hush poems. Those truths are mysterious, yes, and so poems will need an element of mystery. But let the mystery feel necessary—let it feel inescapable. To my ear, to my personality, Merwin's mysteriousness seems like a twenty-four-hour program he can tune into anytime—the Mystery Channel. The reliability of such a program tends to give a poet a highly marketable brand. (John Ashbery, Charles Simic, and Charles Wright have their own spots on the dial.) Poets I admire tend to be more agitated, strenuous, tonally various, unsuave, ironically self-aware. But, as people say in workshops, maybe that's just me.

V / Michael Theune

In the flurry of good-spirited, collegial e-mails that surround this published exchange, Mark Halliday kindly offered me the last word in this dialogue. As the guy who kept sticking his chin out for Halliday's hooks, I'm happy to take the last shot.

However, I don't want to say anything about the substance of Halliday's claims beyond stating that I think many of his points are—of course—worth considering. I certainly will continue to think about them even after this exchange is complete. Instead, where Halliday ends with a discussion of personality and taste, I would like to briefly mention context.

Reader, I am forty-one. Though long aware of and casually acquainted with Merwin's work, I engaged in a close, sustained investigation of it only fairly recently. While initially a drawback—the prolific Merwin gave me a lot of catching up to do—I am very glad to have come to Merwin's work when I did: this allowed me to read him specifically in the context of contemporary poetry, and, frankly, I immediately found his work to be superior to a great deal of it.

While this is perhaps not terribly surprising—after all, Merwin is the US Poet Laureate as I write this—I specifically found Merwin's poetry to be much more significant than much of the poetry produced and marketed under the name "hybrid," a kind of poetry that attempts to meld lyric tradition and avant-garde experiment. I have been engaged in a critique of hybrid poetics for some time, and so, paradoxically, I have been reading a great deal of hybrid poetry over the past decade. I have found that while the synthesis toward which hybridity aims may be a worthwhile goal, one of the key problems with hybridity is that it offers no standard by which to judge if a poet has crafted a successful—let alone *great*—hybrid poem rather than a tangle of short circuits; it is virtually impossible to tell whether a hybrid poem is truly accomplished.

Thus, delving into Merwin's oeuvre was a treat—it was fresh air. For despite the fact that a number of hybrid poets contributed essays on Merwin's work as a part of a tribute to him in a special issue of *Many Mountains Moving*, I found his work to be of another kind and quality to the bulk of hybrid writing—Merwin's work seems to me to be clearly accomplished, achieving a reach, depth, and resonance that much hybrid poetry does not. Especially read in the context of merely *au courant* hybridity, Merwin instantly seemed, and continues to seem, to be a significantly hybrid poet, one who, as I stated earlier in this exchange, successfully combines poetry's orphic and rhetorical tasks and goals.

Merwin is not the only great poet, or the only producer of great poems, in our time. But I do think he is one of them.

In their introduction to *W. S. Merwin: Essays on the Poetry*, Ed Folsom and Cary Nelson state,

> In the debates over a contemporary poet . . . such confidence [in one's evaluative judgments] is often comical, since rival claims that are mutually exclusive exist simultaneously. At its best, that is the risk and perhaps the excitement of judging contemporary poetry—the risk that our readings are subject at every moment to complete deflation. At its worst, evaluation then seems little more than a local effect of the dynamics of power. But that does not make it ungenerous, demonic, or trivial. For it is part of the culture's effort to define who we are and who we may become.[36]

Whatever the evaluations, I do think we'll be talking about Merwin's work for some time, even as the time of its writing recedes into that wild, living thing we conveniently call the past. And I hope consideration of Merwin's poetry stays a part of the effort to define what American poetry is, was, and might become. But of course, yes, maybe that's just me.

All of Memory Waking
Word and Experience in W. S. Merwin's
The Shadow of Sirius

Jerry Harp

Language encodes vast stores of human experience, passed along as we use words in our everyday discourses and our artistic and other cultural pursuits. W. S. Merwin states as much in his 2006 interview with Jeanie Thompson and Jonathan Weinert, included in this volume: "Every word as we use it is completely our own, and yet it's not ours. We didn't invent it. It has a history that we don't know, which contains felt experience from many other lives and many other occasions, from every other time it's been used. So a word is in process of evolution all the time, and yet it's unique to that moment." Even the most intimate of personal statements, if it is to be understood by others, must be articulated in a public language; and this language necessarily carries a long history of associations that have been created by countless others through history and even prehistory. As George Steiner puts it, "A sentence always means more."[1] The sentence itself is never simply the sentence itself, for every word—bearing its history of associations—exceeds the speaker's consciousness. If we had to think out and establish the full meaning of every word, rendering each one completely explicit with each utterance, verbal communication would be either trivial or impossible.

But precisely because language is a public structure, it carries the individual consciousness outside itself. As one scholar of these matters has put it, "[W]e don't have any completely private thoughts."[2] Because human thinking occurs only in the context of the public structures of language, even the most private of thoughts are in some sense cast toward articulation. Thus, as human thinking emerges from the unconscious, it is pulled into consciousness and beyond (into public statement) by the dynamics of language; and as human thinking is pulled into consciousness, it articulates in relationship to the "felt experience from many other lives and many other occasions" encoded in language.

In discussing such dynamics as these, Robert K. Logan has referred to words as "strange attractors" of vast arrays of human experience and perception.[3] In other words, a given word absorbs into itself a great store of sense experience: "A word is a strange attractor for all the percepts associated with the concept represented by that word. A word, therefore, packs a great deal of experience into a single utterance or sign."[4] Consider, for example, all of the generations of experience and observation, going back to our earliest prehistoric ancestors, that were needed to isolate the idea of a tree or cloud or star. These remote roots of our language are of course unrecoverable, though it seems fair to reflect for a moment on what this process could have been. For reasons surely related to survival, it would have been important to take note of various characteristics of the landscape, as well as to notice that certain parts of the landscape bore similarities to each other (and could therefore be referred to as instances of the same thing) and could be counted on to provide—if one found the right ones—food, shade, and shelter. These *trees* could then be used as hiding places for hunting, though they could also function as hiding places for predators of humans, so one would have to approach them with caution. The associations would continue to multiply. Part of the strangeness of these strange attractors is the way they continue to take on associations and meanings as human experience continues to expand. Thus, the image of the tree becomes important in terms of the tree of life, the tree of knowledge of good and evil, the family tree, the gallows tree, and on and on.

A similar reflection could be carried out with regard to the stars of the night sky, which have themselves gathered in stores of human experience in terms of the stories that generations of generations have attributed to them, giving rise to the constellations and their associated lore. These stories themselves become strange attractors as more and more human experience, observation, insight, and reflection come to bear on them. These stories and this lore become a kind of shadow accompanying the given star or constellation. I take this significance of "shadow" as one meaning of the title of W. S. Merwin's *The Shadow of Sirius* (2008), a book much concerned with the stores of human experience that are passed along through language—not individual words alone but those combinations of words that we call stories and poems as well, along with the images and perceptions associated with them.[5] As Merwin puts it in the poem "Nocturne," "The stars emerge one / by one into the names / that were last found for them." The names remain plural, and the stars "emerge . . . into" them, meaning that word and perception merge. The meaning becomes a part of the thing, a shadow that always accompanies it.

The *shadow* of Sirius—the brightest star in the night sky—is composed of the stories, lore, and ideas that have become intertwined with it. Much of what has come to be associated with this star is well recounted in Jay B. Holberg's marvelous *Sirius: Brightest Diamond in the Night Sky* (2007). Sirius is especially fit for a consideration of this merging of name and thing, lore and perception, for it has figured prominently in the mythologies of many cultures. In ancient Egypt the reappearance of Sirius in the morning sky, after seventy days out of sight, anticipated the annual flooding of the Nile. The star was the "heavenly representation of Isis," who was "associated with the giving of life, the fecundity of nature and nurturing." It was also associated with Hathor—who, "like Isis, was a goddess of love, but a love more focused on fertility"—as well as the myth of the phoenix. In ancient Greece it was associated with "heat, fire, and even fevers," as well as "dogs, and in some instances with the ominous presence of doom." It may not be entirely coincidental that in China Sirius "is known as *Tsien Lang* or the Heavenly Wolf." Today we know Sirius as the major star of the constellation Canis Major, the Greater Dog in Latin, thus revealing the influence of ancient Rome on the lore associated with the star. Along with Canis Minor, the Lesser Dog, Canis Major accompanies the hunter Orion.[6]

As I take Merwin's title to imply, Sirius is shadowed by these rich associations, but in modern times we have come to know more about the shadow of Sirius in yet another sense, the much dimmer star, known as Sirius B, locked in orbit with it. Together Sirius (also known as Sirius A) and Sirius B form a binary star system, that is, two stars that orbit each other. Sometimes the two stars in such a system orbit so closely together that it takes some time for astronomers to discern that they are in fact seeing two stars instead of one.[7] In fact, Sirius B is sufficiently dim that it took astronomers years to discern that it was even there. In the past, however, Sirius B was the brighter of the two; over time it grew dim and was lost in the glare of its companion star.[8] Thus, the two together form a vivid metaphor of the associations that may accompany a given thing—whether a word, a star, or a tree—even if the associations have receded into shadow. At any given moment, we may not be fully aware of all that accompanies a given thing, but the shadows of these earlier associations remain present; we need only work to discern them. In *The Shadow of Sirius*, Merwin explores quite explicitly the significance of this work of discernment, as the poems display an exquisite sensitivity to the words that speak us as we speak them, carrying along the generations of experience implicit in them.

The opening poem of the collection, "The Nomad Flute," invokes an instance of such experience carried along implicitly in a work of art. The title alludes to *Eighteen Songs of a Nomad Flute*, about the Chinese poet Cai Wenji of the Han Dynasty (202 BCE–220 CE), who was kidnapped by the nomadic Xiongnu people and forced to marry a tribal chief.[9] The poems tell her story among her captors, her bearing of two children to the tribal chief, and her eventual return to her own people.[10] Although the poems we have today were written in the eighth century by the poet Liu Shang, they are cast in Cai Wenji's voice. In Merwin's poem the flute is a figure of the poet herself, and thus it functions metonymically as the poet's language—the words of the poet are produced by the artist's breath, as are the sounds of the flute. The poem addresses Cai Wenji, who has spoken across the centuries:

> You that sang to me once sing to me now
> let me hear your long lifted note
> survive with me
> the star is fading

Produced by the artist's breath, her "long lifted note," mediated by the text that recounts her song, breathes into the present-day poet, enabling him to breathe creatively also. In the fourth poem of *Eighteen Songs of a Nomad Flute*, the exile, gazing at the moon and longing for her home, utters, "In my half-dreaming state is it possible that some messages may be transmitted?" Merwin's poem holds out the possibility that the answer is yes, that he does in fact hear "messages" from the ancient past. The printed text encodes the sounded words, which become the events carrying the poem's experience. The fading star in the lines quoted above may allude to the star of the book's title, in whose shadow the opening ritual of this poem is enacted. The light coming from this star is something that these two poets share across centuries, though its fading also calls to mind the passing of time that keeps them apart. In this realm of the intersecting of poets and their poetry, the contemporary speaker holds out the possibility that his ancient counterpart might in some sense encounter him also, for they share something of this "half-dreaming state":

> do you still hear me
> does your air
> remember you
> o breath of morning
> night song morning song
> I have with me
> all that I do not know
> I have lost none of it

The poet of the past still breathes because the modern poet reads her, encountering her breath alive still in these marks on the page. Her song, circulating in the world, has become the "breath of morning." And it is because her words—or rather, the words her story inspired—carry experiences that this speaker has not directly had that he can say, "I have with me / all that I do not know." These experiences inform his own experience as a nomad, not in a literal sense but rather in the sense that all humans are nomads, traveling the earth for a brief span, never entirely at home, at least not as long as we remain alive. The line "night song morning song" alludes to the Divine Office, the ritual prayers consisting largely of psalms and biblical canticles, at the heart of certain traditions of monastic life. It is a life that approaches experience in the world as nomadic, a journey. The poem works in part as an invitation to the reader to accompany the poet on some portion of this journey, as the poet accompanies Cai Wenji in her nomadic exile.

"The Nomad Flute" is indeed followed by a night song and then a morning song. The former, "Blueberries after Dark," begins, "So this is the way the night tastes." The experience is one of the world as registered on the tongue, a gustatory sense of the darkness. The taste leads, in Proustian fashion, to the speaker's recollection of his mother telling him "that I was not afraid of the dark." This recollection of darkness, which he can enter because he has recalled his mother's reassuring words, along with this taste of darkness, leads to a litany of the dead: the speaker's maternal grandfather, his maternal grandmother, and then his great-grandmother, uncle, and brother. But all of these deaths are stated in relationship to his mother: "her father," "her mother," "her grandmother," "her only brother," "her firstborn." The taste of the blueberries brings him within intimate precincts of his mother's experiences of loss. The subtext of the poem is the speaker's own loss of his mother, whose experiences of loss he inherits. The poem also by implication anticipates the speaker's own coming entry into the darkness of death.

The morning song that follows, "Still Morning," alludes to the dawn of the speaker's life. In attempting to create the sense of childhood timelessness, when "there is only one / age and it knows / nothing of age," he states, "I am a child before there are words." But once he utters these words, the illusory moment of preverbal wholeness is shattered, for he is always already recalling or creating this moment in a state of fallenness into language. He partakes here of what Wordsworth calls, in the "Intimations Ode" (line 189), the "philosophic mind," the intimate recollection of preverbal childhood experience depending on the very conceptual apparatus that distances one from the world. In this case, the language of the poem enables access to a memory in which "arms are holding me up in a shadow" and he watches "one patch of sunlight moving / across the green carpet." But even though the voices of the past are silent now, the poem's words enact a moment of recollection enlivened into the present, "while I go on seeing that patch of sunlight." The visionary moment remains a gift from the past, carrying a whole sense of the world and the speaker's integration with it.

As this poem reminds us, human memory is always a matter of mediation; it is never entirely direct. The poem thus creates a scene of the innocent consciousness entering into the fragmenting realm of language and the arrays of experience that it carries. Although this language separates consciousness from the world, it is this separation that allows human consciousness to exist at all. The fall into language is a fortunate fall as one learns of and experiences loss, for one is able to be aware of this loss, to be in conscious attendance—in mediated form—on one's recollections, and to create art from the past facing the future. As the poem "Note" puts it,

> Remember how the naked soul
> comes to language and at once knows
> loss and distance and believing

The speech-act of command ("Remember") calls attention to how the idea of the naked soul coming into language must be constructed in retrospect, even if it is created out of the fragments and residue of sense experience. The remembered scene remains a mediated construct—which is not to say that the memory thus created does not carry great truth, but rather that it is a construction of self-reflective consciousness. The realm of memory is the realm that language has already infiltrated. But once the image is created, it can resonate sufficiently with one's experience of the world to indicate that it carries something of veracity.

In the memory that this speaker constructs, the once naked soul, having entered the losses and distances of language, will also

> hearken to how
> one story becomes another
> and will try to tell where
> they have emerged from

This "note" to the reader functions itself as an instance of the very dynamic that it describes, for it is a story about where all stories have emerged from—the experience of the once "naked soul," having fallen into language, seeking to negotiate its experience of loss and its yearning even as it looks ahead to where "they [these stories] are heading." But because it is facing into the future where the stories have not yet arrived, this soul finds itself at a loss, for there is not yet a narrative to make sense of what has not yet occurred—"running before the words and beyond them / naked and never looking back // through the noise of questions." The soul's nakedness is a kind of recovered nakedness, the nakedness of the philosophic mind, for it has not yet formed a language to say what the future story is, though it is exquisitely aware of itself. The poem does not imply that there are no answers to the questions the soul encounters, but rather that one does well at times to run ahead of the "noise" of their words. The words do indeed serve, and they do so partly by pointing toward the silence that they have emerged from—a silence rendered more meaningful to human consciousness by the words that one speaks—and back into which they subside.

Further, as the poet reminds us in "Recognitions," "Stories come to us like new senses." Stories not only make sense experience vivid and memorable but also build our sense experiences into a meaningful world. Without the constructions of narrative, sense experiences remain one sensation after another; the narrative provides coherence and meaning. At the same time, the narratives by which we make sense of our experiences may disclose a new sense of the world, one that was hitherto merely inchoate in human consciousness: "a view of the world we could not have guessed at // but that we always wanted to believe." The implied paradox of these lines is that what we have longed to believe is also what we could not have articulated for ourselves until we discovered it in the implications of the stories that we tell. The stories articulate a sense of the world that we can recognize as our own even though we could not have realized it without the stories. As the poem implies, one of the great functions of literature is to provide such narratives to prompt us to recognize the world in terms that we have longed for but could not have known without them.

That words carry their own distinctive associations, encodings of human experience, and senses of the world is well known to any devoted reader. As Merwin has said, words take on distinctive shadings as they are used over a long period and become dense with meaning and personal nuances. Such gathering in of meaning comes to the fore in "The Long and Short of It," about the human belief in *measure*, a term related to "metrical or rhythmical value"; such value has a long history in the traditions of poetry.[11] "As long as we can believe anything," begins the poem, "we believe in measure":

> we do it with the first breath we take
> and the first sound we make
> it is in each word we learn

The nouns of this passage progress from breath (the basic function of living) to sound (as in the lalling stage, in which the infant begins to play with sounds, moving toward the articulation of language), to speech (the production of words). Congruently, the actions marked out for each stage progress from taking to making to learning. As the child grows to turn breath into words, he or she both makes meaning and learns new possibilities of meaning.

To learn carries deep etymological roots relating to *lore*. To learn means to participate in the lore of a tradition, fundamentally by means of the measures of articulated language. As the poem goes on to recount, this sense of measure connects with the recurrences woven into human experience, as in rituals surrounding food, as well as in associations inscribed in the celestial regions: "it is there in *meal* and in *moon*" (italics in original). Further,

> in *meaning* it is the meaning
> it is the firmament and the furrow
> turning at the end of the field
> and the verse turning with its breath
> it is in memory that keeps telling us
> some of the old story about us

The word *meaning* has roots in ideas of love, affection, and agreement. What one means by "meaning," then, relates to human relations, as well as to the experience of breathing. Similarly, the poem relates the articulation of human experience in verse to the plowing of fields. Indeed, the Latin root of "verse," *versus*, means "a line or row," specifically "a line of writing (so named from turning to begin another line)," and it is an ancient commonplace to associate the turning of verse with the turning of a plow in the

field.[12] Thus, the poem finds the roots of poetry in breathing, human rela-
tions and rituals, and plowing—three of the most basic of human activities,
the most recent of which (plowing) developed in the Neolithic era. These
ancient practices have helped to form the measure of human identity and
community.

Words, which are the music of human consciousness and cognition, func-
tion as "parts of a tune." In the poem of this title, the speaker describes an
old man humming some notes of a song "he thought he had forgotten." The
notes encode associations that precede even his own memory, of the

> days when as he knows there was
> no word for *life* in the language
> and if they wanted to say *eyes* or *heart*
> they would hold up a leaf . . .

One can only guess—at least *I* can only guess—why the leaf would work
this way, as a strange attractor carrying associations with eyes and the
heart. The associations may have to do with the mere shapes of leaves,
some of which resemble eyes, others hearts. It may be that this phylogenic
memory, recovered from the distant past, exists only in fragments. What
meanings might flash across the mind are indeed only fleeting, the way
"birds carried water in their voices." The poem ends with the figure of the
old man enraptured by this sheer evanescence of sound: "and as he sits
there humming he remembers / some of the words they come back to him
now / he smiles hearing them come and go." "Sound exists only when it is
going out of existence," and thus our spoken words are themselves sheer
evanescence, reminders that our structures of meaning exist in time and
are always passing away. We need such stories as Merwin writes as lasting
reminders that nothing in our world is lasting.[13]

The world as we know it has to pass away if anything new is to occur.
The book's closing poem, "The Laughing Thrush," brings together an ap-
preciation of the past and an anticipation and welcoming of what is to
come, even as it queries the possibility of a future, for the present moment
remains precariously balanced: "the words that lately have fallen silent /
to surface among the phrases of some future / if there is a future." And
yet the poem is a hymn of welcome to the morning, the "nameless joy of

morning," which has "all of memory waking into it." The morning here celebrated brings with it the possibility of the new. An assurance of mere repetition of the same would sound a deadening note. In its welcoming of uncertainty, the poem faces into the unknown, the only future available to human experience.

The Form of Absence

David Caplan

A poetic form is typically defined by its characteristics. Following this sensible commonplace, the *Princeton Encyclopedia of Poetry and Poetics* defines Western culture's dominant poetic form, the sonnet, according to its length ("a 14-line poem"), customary meters (hendecasyllables, alexandrines, and iambic pentameter for Italian, French, and English respectively), and "traditional rhyme schemes."[1] Notwithstanding the many variations of the popular form, its varieties and subvarieties, the "clearest modern definition"[2] relies on these elements. Forms not easily defined in this way inspire a certain critical unease, if not hostility. When T. S. Eliot attacked free verse, he did so by charging that it failed a related test. "If *vers libre* is a genuine verse-form," Eliot maintained, "it will have a positive definition. And I can define it only in negatives: (1) absence of pattern, (2) absence of rhyme, (3) absence of metre."[3] Eliot's pointed language asserts a neat contrast. He condemns free verse for lacking a specific affirmative quality; to underscore the point, he repeats the word "absence" as a taunt. Accordingly, free verse suffers from a dire lack. In this respect, Eliot follows Doctor Johnson's slighting of blank verse—metrical poetry defined by an absence of rhyme—as simply "blank."[4]

An alternative challenge that a form faces is whether the form generates other poems, whether it serves as a useful model, not an idiosyncratic experiment. In this respect, the accuracy of the literary history that drives the poem remains less important than its attractiveness, its inspirational value. A form might start a literary craze; less noisily and more lastingly, it might inspire other poems so successfully that subsequent poets use the form without having in mind the earlier practitioners. In the latter case, the form often loses a certain self-consciousness as it develops into one of a number that the culture makes available to authors. For instance, a decade after his death, many ghazals in English bear the influence of Agha Shahid Ali, whereas many recent sestinas show little recognition of any precursors in the form, little recognition of the form's long history. (Few recent poems in either form suggest much awareness of the forms' rich traditions in languages other than English.) This otherwise regrettable ignorance offers a certain benefit; in some cases, it helps forms to flourish as they accommodate new concerns and motivations.

Starting in the 1960s, W. S. Merwin removed punctuation from his poems, defending his practice in several often-cited interviews. "[A]nything you do as a condition of a poem," he asserted, "becomes a form by itself. If you stop using punctuation, that's a kind of formality."[5] In Merwin's poetry, the lack of punctuation achieves a range of effects. Most strikingly, it recasts the terms of Eliot's dismissal of free verse; Merwin crafts a form defined by absence. Merwin's example has been quietly successful; the form he developed influenced poets whose work shows a deep knowledge of his poetry and some poets whose work does not. In this essay I will discuss two poets from the former camp and one from the latter. My aim is to give a sense of Merwin's formal influence, to suggest the varied effects that poets of different temperaments achieve when they draw from his work.

◆ ◆ ◆

A grave solemnity haunts many poems in Merwin's 2008 collection, *The Shadow of Sirius*, winner of the Pulitzer Prize for Poetry in 2009. Negative propositions abound, evoking a disquieting sense of unfulfilled longing. "[A]pparently we believe / in the words," one poem observes, "but we long beyond them / for what is unseen / what remains out of reach."[6] Grammar and metaphysics are one; both dramatize what remains neither seen nor grasped. The poem most focused on this notion, "No," takes its title from a negative proposition. The poem explores what it negates:

Out at the end of the street in the cemetery
the tombstones stared across the wheeling shadows
of tombstones while the names and dates wept on
in full daylight and behind them where the hill
sheared off two rusted tracks under a black
iron gate led up out of pure darkness
and the unbroken sound of pure darkness
that went on all the time under everything
not breathing beneath the sounds of breathing
but no they said it was not the entrance
to the underworld or anything like that
in fact all the houses along the street
had been paid for by what had come from there
in the days of the negatives of the pictures

Images of erasure and effacement dominate the lines and their construction; three consecutive lines, for example, end with "black," "pure darkness," and "pure darkness." Two other lines include three instances of "no" and its cognates, in addition to one negative conjunction: "*not* breathing beneath the sounds of breathing / *but no* they said it was *not* the entrance." In one respect, the poem shows punctuation to be syntactically unnecessary; an attentive reader does not need these markers in order to grasp the sentences or their relation, let alone to perceive the poem's formal elegance. Instead, the absence of punctuation achieves a deeply expressive effect. The poem moves fluidly between the living and dead; it affirms the connection it denies. What, for instance, would inspire the unnamed speakers to assert, "it was not the entrance / to the underworld"? Buried with this odd denial is the belief that an entrance to the underworld exists and the suspicion that this cemetery might serve as one, regardless of what the speakers say. The punning last line reinforces this presence of absence; the negatives persist.

Merwin's elimination of punctuation also recasts literary history. For expediency's sake, I will summarize a popular narrative about the field. The most familiar accountings of twentieth- and twenty-first-century literary history associate techniques such as unconventional typography and punctuation with determinedly avant-garde verse. Inspired by new technologies, intellectual developments, and cultural shifts, poets incorporate new techniques into their poetry, signaling their responsiveness to contemporary life. To the unsympathetic observer, though, these techniques reveal a modish superficiality. In a classic denunciation of Modernist formal experimentation, Robert Frost disdainfully observed: "The one old way to be new no longer served. Science put it into our heads that there must be new ways to be new. Those tried were largely by subtraction—elimination. Poetry, for example, was tried without punctuation."[7]

Merwin's poetry inverts the terms of this debate. In interviews, Merwin often describes punctuation as a modern invention imposed on poetry but fitting for prose: "[I]t was really invented in the seventeenth century for prose. Not for poetry at all."[8] Drawing from this different appreciation of punctuation's role in poetry and prose, his poetry claims a certain timeless quality. Even when depicting specifically contemporary scenes, it evokes a longer historical perspective. When Merwin tells us that "where the hill / sheared off two rusted tracks under a black / iron gate led up out of pure darkness," in image and style the lines suggest the contemporary moment perceived from the viewpoint of "pure darkness," a moment both in and outside the depicted time.

In certain cases Merwin exerts a clear influence on other writers, one easily documented in both poetry and prose. In addition to his own poetry collections, H. L. Hix, for instance, published *Understanding W. S. Merwin*. Introducing his motivation for writing the critical study, Hix calls Merwin his "yardstick for the language."[9] In his chapter devoted to the subject, though, Hix objects to Merwin's love poetry. His aggrieved tone betrays a great admirer's disappointment:

> In a world ruled by a beneficent god or one where human society consistently progresses, love may be a sufficient force to redeem the world. But in a tragic world, in which malevolent or indifferent forces more powerful than ourselves influence human activity, love, no matter how strong, cannot redeem the world. If lovers can be parted by forces they cannot control, such as death, love may be a consolation, but it cannot provide security. If the world is tragic . . . love does not keep it from being tragic.[10]

Citing what he calls "the incompatibility between love and Merwin's tragic vision," Hix sees Merwin's love poetry as "a weakness throughout his mature books," since Merwin "treats it [love] as magical escape."[11] Hix's most searching explorations of this issue, though, occur in his own poetry. Consider the following section of Hix's sequence "The Well-Tempered Clavier":

> the gods keep to themselves even here
> we hear them yes but in whispers inscrutably
> like voices in another room less heard than intuited
> the gods keep to themselves everywhere
> their mumbling indistinct between gusts of wind
> sometimes the living are spirits too
> they speak in flashes of light we see them from the corners of our eyes
> there are no souls but there are voices
> there are nights the crickets make sense
> sometimes even the insects are spirits
> don't try to name this voice don't try to locate it
> the answer to all your questions about it is yes
> is it from your wife yes is it from her lover yes
> is it from your own bad conscience yes
> is it from god yes of course the devil yes the devil too
> is it from the dead yes from the boy you once picked a fight with yes
> the first girl you loved yes the first you betrayed yes was she the same
>   of course
> from those who trusted you yes those who knew better yes
> from the part of you that knew every piece of this long ago yes yes[12]

This passage could not have been written without Merwin. Most obviously, Merwin's work serves as a formal model. Both the cadences of Hix's lines and their lack of punctuation express a familiar timelessness, a being in and out of time. Yet Hix adds his own characteristic obsessions to this influence. Rather perversely, the poem advises, "don't try to name this voice don't try to locate it," but the line both admonishes and tempts the reader to do exactly that. When introduced to a "voice," a reader tries to name and locate it. In this respect, the chastisement simply increases the desire.

Published nearly a decade before "No," Hix's lines read like a rewriting of that poem, with each affirmation expressing a deeper negation: "is it from your wife yes is it from her lover yes / is it from your own bad conscience yes." Relentlessly the poem returns to the concerns that drove Hix as a reader of Merwin. The poem catalogs the "malevolent or indifferent forces more powerful than ourselves [that] influence human activity": it depicts indifferent gods, unfaithful husbands, and unfaithful wives, who share only a bad conscience. From our first experience of it, to love is to betray. The lines dramatize what Hix finds lacking in Merwin's work: an understanding that love cannot redeem this tragic world. Hix writes the love poem he wishes Merwin had written.

In her collection *Fimbul-Winter*, Debra Allbery also turns to Merwin, but with a technician's appreciation. "After Vermeer" incorporates Merwin's "Elegy"; an endnote acknowledges the debt in case an inattentive reader missed it. In the same collection, the unpunctuated poem "Office" describes a speaker walking into an office building:

> she sits and presses
> power buttons on and on their wheezed whirring
> like a scour a spun erasing inside her those
> loosed leaves somewhere still scribbling something
> she used to know how to read[13]

The poem contrasts two worlds: the world outside the office building and the world inside. The dry leaves might offer a bleak image, but the office doors seal off even that meager sign of vitality: "spiraling then scattering their last rasp behind her." Instead, the unpunctuated poem shows how this unforgiving landscape strips away the speaker's humanity, concluding with a kind of double negative: an image of a machine erasing from inside the speaker something already erased: "loosed leaves somewhere still scribbling something / she used to know how to read." This image links vitality with nature and technology with dehumanization. While the "loosed leaves" suggest freedom, the "power buttons" the speaker presses rob her of her power. Nature remains the source of creativity and self-preservation; to retain a sense of self, the speaker must retain a connection with the world outside the office building.

While the setting updates these classic Romantic portrayals of nature, self, and creativity, the unpunctuated form adds another effect. Forcefully the unpunctuated lines dramatize the desire and need for connection, a resistance to closing off parts of the self. The final image laments the speaker's inability to connect with language, creativity, and her own self. It laments all she has lost. Like "loosed leaves," though, language spills across the barriers erected in the poem, retaining a counter-energy. The unpunctuated lines resist the separations they depict.

Hix and Allbery openly acknowledge Merwin as an influence. In contrast, Eve Grubin draws from Merwin less directly and frequently; only one of her poems shows this influence and does so obliquely. A different sensibility inspires her poetry, partly because of notably different life experiences. Merwin grew up the son of a Presbyterian minister and later studied Zen Buddhism; Hix is the only member of his evangelical family not to retain that faith. Emphasizing this connection, in the first words of his introduction to *Understanding W. S. Merwin* he suggests that the "[m] any notable writers" who "grew up in religious households" share a certain kinship. "Characteristics of the household in which he was raised," Hix adds, "pervade Merwin's work and help create his distinctive voice." Grubin's work draws from a different life trajectory. She did not grow up in a religious household; as an adult she chose those structures of practice and belief. Accordingly, she writes as a Jew increasingly drawn to Orthodox Judaism.

"Date," for instance, describes not just any date but one conducted under specific conditions. The couple meets in a "meat / restaurant,"[14] that is, a kosher restaurant, presumably a little more upscale than a dairy restaurant. Markers of religious and secular Judaism commingle, as in the conversation where the couple discusses Bernard Malamud, the twentieth-century Jewish-American novelist, and Rashi, the eleventh-century biblical and Talmudic commentator. Rooted in a particular religious culture, the poem returns to its elements. Specific notions of modesty and physical intimacy govern how the speaker and her date dress and act. The couple will not touch each other, and their clothes reveal little uncovered flesh, a fact that intensifies the experience of looking and seeing:

> his eyes
>
> regarding the skin just above my clavicle rain
> plunged hard behind his round glasses and black skullcap

These lines do not aspire to Merwin's formal elegance; they embody an urgent intensity. Like the look they describe, they are troubled and over-heated. As Merwin noted of his own poetry, the lack of punctuation serves as "a formality." Grubin's poetry approaches the same form differently. In essence her unpunctuated lines dramatize a stripping bare, as the smallest gestures reveal the exact nature of desire, a shocking intimacy. The phrase "meat / restaurant" specifies a kind of kosher establishment, the proper separation of certain food groups, but the line break shearing adjective from noun reinforces the physicality of all involved, the force of their bodies' demands. Grubin's poem differs from Merwin's in setting and concerns; no reader would confuse their poetry. She is a reader of his work, not a devotee. In response to my query, Grubin observed: "I have always read and admired Merwin's poems but I don't think I was conscious of his work when I wrote the poem 'The Date.' . . . The poem does not seem to have much in common with Merwin although perhaps the lack of punctuation in his work allowed other poets to consciously or unconsciously be more open to doing away with punctuation."[15]

Grubin's more tenuous connection to Merwin's work suggests a wider development. The lack of punctuation does not remain limited to a specific set of thematic concerns or effects, whether approached in agreement or contestation. Instead, Merwin's model makes quite different work possible. It inspires a range of poems, not just those which bear the most visible marks of influence. The lack of punctuation develops beyond an individual style. It serves as a form, a flexible means of ordering language, open to new experiences and artistic temperaments.

Notes

The Names of the Trees Where I Was Born / Weinert

1. W. S. Merwin, *A Mask for Janus* (New Haven, CT: Yale University Press, 1952).

2. Richard Howard, *Alone with America: Essays on the Art of Poetry in the United States since 1950* (New York: Atheneum, 1980), 443.

3. W. S. Merwin, *Green with Beasts* (New York: Alfred A. Knopf, 1956).

4. Howard, *Alone with America*, 427.

5. W. S. Merwin, *Writings to an Unfinished Accompaniment* (New York: Atheneum, 1973).

6. W. S. Merwin, *The Rain in the Trees* (New York: Alfred A. Knopf, 1988).

7. W. S. Merwin, *The Moving Target* (New York: Atheneum, 1963).

8. Howard, *Alone with America*, 435.

9. W. S. Merwin, *The Lice* (New York: Atheneum, 1967).

10. W. S. Merwin, *The Carrier of Ladders* (New York: Atheneum, 1970).

11. Helen Vendler, "Desolation Shading into Terror," *New York Times*, October 18, 1970, 28.

12. Ibid., 30.

13. W. S. Merwin, *Regions of Memory: Uncollected Prose, 1949–82*, ed. Ed Folsom and Cary Nelson (Urbana: University of Illinois Press, 1987), 336.

14. Wallace Stevens, *The Collected Poems of Wallace Stevens* (New York: Alfred A. Knopf, 1980), 328.

15. Merwin, *Regions of Memory*, 336–37.

16. "Air," from *The Moving Target*, is widely viewed as the *ars poetica* of Merwin's early poetry. In that poem the speaker walks along a road at night on an unspecified journey whose end is endlessly deferred: "This must be what I wanted to be doing, / Walking at night between the two deserts, / Singing."

17. W. S. Merwin, *The Compass Flower* (New York: Atheneum, 1977).

18. W. S. Merwin, *Finding the Islands* (San Francisco: North Point Press, 1982).

19. W. S. Merwin, *Opening the Hand* (New York: Atheneum, 1983).

20. Folsom in Merwin, *Regions of Memory*, 327.

21. Charles Altieri, "Situating Merwin's Poetry since 1970," in *W. S. Merwin: Essays on the Poetry*, ed. Ed Folsom and Cary Nelson (Urbana: University of Illinois Press, 1987), 175.

22. Ibid., 161.

23. W. S. Merwin, *Unframed Originals* (New York: Atheneum, 1982).

24. Merwin, *Regions of Memory*, 326.

25. Merwin, *Unframed Originals*, 56.

26. W. S. Merwin, *The Drunk in the Furnace* (New York: Macmillan, 1960).

27. Edward Brunner, "*Opening the Hand*: The Variable Caesura and the Family Poems," in *W. S. Merwin*, ed. Folsom and Nelson, 287.

28. W. S. Merwin, *Travels* (New York: Alfred A. Knopf, 1993).

29. W. S. Merwin, *The Folding Cliffs* (New York: Alfred A. Knopf, 1998).

30. Dante, *Purgatorio*, trans. W. S. Merwin (New York: Alfred A. Knopf, 2000).

31. W. S. Merwin, "A Reading by U.S. Poet Laureate W. S. Merwin," Phillips Academy, Andover, MA, May 6, 2011.

To Merwin / Spaar

1. W. S. Merwin, *A Mask for Janus* (New Haven, CT: Yale University Press, 1954).

2. W. S. Merwin, *Present Company* (Port Townsend, WA: Copper Canyon, 2005).

3. W. S. Merwin, *The Lice* (New York: Atheneum, 1967).

4. Richard Howard, *Alone with America: Essays on the Art of Poetry in*

the United States since 1950 (New York: Atheneum, 1980), 419, 442, 437.

5. Ibid., 448; Helen Vendler, *Part of Nature, Part of Us: Modern American Poets* (Cambridge, MA: Harvard University Press, 1980), 235.

6. Carl Phillips, "The Ode," in *Radiant Lyre: Essays on Lyric Poetry*, ed. David Baker and Ann Townsend (St. Paul, MN: Graywolf, 2007), 91.

7. Howard, *Alone with America*, 336.

8. Stanley Plumly, "Between Things: On the Ode," in *Radiant Lyre*, ed. Baker and Townsend, 113–15.

9. Thomas Wyatt, *The Essential Wyatt*, ed. W. S. Merwin (New York: Ecco, 1989).

10. Plumly, "Between Things," 115–16.

11. Phillips, "Ode," 92.

Origin, Presence, and Time / Irwin

1. W. S. Merwin, *Present Company* (Port Townsend, WA: Copper Canyon, 2005).

2. W. S. Merwin, *Green with Beasts* (New York: Alfred A. Knopf, 1956).

3. W. S. Merwin, *Dancing Bears* (New York: Alfred A. Knopf, 1954).

4. W. S. Merwin, "The House and Garden: The Emergence of a Dream," *Kenyon Review* 32, no. 4 (Fall 2010): 14.

5. W. S. Merwin, "A Conversation with W. S. Merwin," interview by Mark Irwin, *Many Mountains Moving* 4, no. 2 (2000): 47.

6. Aristotle, *Poetics*, trans. Ingram Bywater (New York: Random House, 1954).

7. Emmanuel Levinas, *Otherwise Than Being*, trans. Alphonso Lingis (Pittsburgh: Duquesne University Press, 2006), 150.

8. W. S. Merwin, *The Shadow of Sirius* (Port Townsend, WA: Copper Canyon, 2008).

9. W. S. Merwin, *The Rain in the Trees* (New York: Alfred A. Knopf, 1988).

10. W. S. Merwin, *The Lice* (New York: Atheneum, 1967).

11. Henry David Thoreau, *The Essays of Henry David Thoreau* (New York: North Point, 2002), 162.

12. W. S. Merwin, *Writings to an Unfinished Accompaniment* (New York: Atheneum, 1973).

13. Merwin, "A Conversation with W. S. Merwin," 52.

14. W. S. Merwin, quoted in Stephen Berg and Robert Mezey, *Naked Poetry* (Indianapolis: Bobbs-Merrill, 1969), 271.

A Forgotten Language / Pankey

1. W. S. Merwin, *The Rain in the Trees* (New York: Alfred A. Knopf, 1988); W. S. Merwin, *The Lice* (New York: Atheneum, 1967).

A Time of Memories Incorrect but Powerful / Dean

1. W. S. Merwin, *The Rain in the Trees* (New York: Alfred A. Knopf, 1988).

2. W. S. Merwin, "Letter on the Wao Kele O Puna Rain Forest," *American Poetry Review* 19, no. 2 (March/April 1990), 43–45. This piece actually consists of two letters, one dated October 1989 and the other January 1990. Wao Kele O Puna was purchased by the Trust for Public Land in 2006 and formally turned over to the Office of Hawaiian Affairs in 2007. It is believed to be the home of Pele, goddess of volcanoes.

3. W. S. Merwin, "A Language for Nature: Preserving the Hawaiian Rainforest," 1992, available at Poets.org, Academy of American Poets: http://www.poets.org/viewmedia.php/prmMID/21635.

4. Readers interested in a broader discussion of these poems may wish to consult Jane Frazier, *From Origin to Ecology: Nature and the Poetry of W. S. Merwin* (Teaneck, NJ: Fairleigh Dickinson University Press, 1999), chap. 5 ("Language and Nature"), and H. L. Hix, *Understanding W. S. Merwin* (Columbia: University of South Carolina Press, 1997), chap. 9 ("Hawaii").

5. Norman Friedman, "Symbol," in *The New Princeton Encyclopedia of Poetry and Poetics*, ed. Alex Preminger and T. V. F. Brogan (Princeton, NJ: Princeton University Press, 1993), 1253.

6. Henry David Thoreau, *Walden: An Annotated Edition*, ed. Walter Harding (Boston: Houghton Mifflin, 1995), 319.

7. "Chord," in *Random House Dictionary*, 2011, Dictionary.com: http://dictionary.reference/browse/chord/.

8. Ibid.

9. *Opening the Hand* was later republished in W. S. Merwin, *Flower and*

Hand: Poems 1977–1983 (Port Townsend, WA: Copper Canyon, 1996).

10. Of the landscape of his childhood Merwin has said, "The Pennsylvania that I grew up in and loved as a child isn't there; I don't mean it's just been developed into suburbs either—it's been strip-mined: it really is literally not there." W. S. Merwin, interview by Ed Folsom, in *Contemporary Authors: New Revised Series 15* (Farmington Hills, MI: Gale, 1985), 323.

11. Robert Frost, quoted in Reginald L. Cook, "Frost on Frost: The Making of Poems," *American Literature* 28, no. 1 (March 1956): 72.

Merwin's Evolving Protocols / Cramer

1. Johann Wolfgang von Goethe, quoted in Paul Goodman, "Advanced-Guard Writing, 1900–1950," *Kenyon Review* 13, no. 3 (Summer 1951), 376.

2. W. S. Merwin, *The Second Four Books of Poems* (Port Townsend, WA: Copper Canyon, 1993).

3. W. S. Merwin, *The Moving Target* (New York: Atheneum, 1963). Purists will object. In the exception that proves the rule, each of the sixty-three lines of "The Last One," from *The Lice* (1967), ends with a period.

4. W. S. Merwin, *Travels* (New York: Alfred A. Knopf, 1993).

5. Paul Breslin, *The Psycho-political Muse: American Poetry since the Fifties* (Chicago: University of Chicago Press, 1987), 131.

6. Ibid., 136.

7. W. S. Merwin, *The Lice* (New York: Atheneum, 1967).

8. W. S. Merwin, *The Rain in the Trees* (New York: Alfred A. Knopf, 1988).

9. W. S. Merwin, *The Lice.*

10. W. S. Merwin, interview by David L. Elliott, *Contemporary Literature* 29, no. 1 (Spring 1988), 16. The neuroscientist would go Merwin one further: the brain itself is an equal, if silent, partner in the process we call perception. "Placing your eyes on something is no guarantee of seeing it," writes David M. Eagleman in *Incognito: The Secret Lives of the Brain* (New York: Pantheon Books, 2011), 26.

11. I favor semicolons for the fourth movement and periods for the fifth because the independent clauses in the former create a sequence of illustrative examples, whereas those in the latter are best appreciated as related, but distinct, declarative sentences.

12. Laurence Lieberman, "Recent Poetry in Review," *Yale Review* 57 (Summer 1968): 597.

13. I've adapted here the title of chapter 6 in Breslin, *Psycho-political Muse*: "Deep Images, Shallow Psychologies: The Unconscious as Pastoral Retreat," 118–35.

14. Ibid., 138.

15. Ibid., 149.

The Act Finds the Utterance / Gander

1. W. S. Merwin, *The Vixen* (New York: Alfred A. Knopf, 1996).

Most of the Stories Have to Do with Vanishing / Zapruder

1. W. S. Merwin, *The Vixen* (New York: Alfred A. Knopf, 1996).

To Shine after It Has Gone / Thompson

1. Thomas Byers, "A Lecture on the Poet W. S. Merwin" (lecture, Spalding University, Louisville, KY, November 2006).

2. W. S. Merwin, *The Vixen* (New York: Alfred A. Knopf, 1996).

3. Richard Howard, "The Vixen," *Boston Review* 21, no. 3 (Summer 1996), http://bostonreview.net/BR21.3/Reviews.html (accessed November 20, 2011).

4. Walter Murch and Michael Ondaatje, *The Conversations: Walter Murch and the Art of Editing Film* (New York: Alfred A. Knopf, 2004), 268.

5. Howard, "The Vixen."

6. W. S. Merwin, interview by John Amen, *Pedestal Magazine* 15 (April–June 2003), http://www.thepedestalmagazine.com/gallery.php?item=703 (accessed September 1, 2011).

7. Howard, "The Vixen."

8. Ibid.

9. W. S. Merwin, interview with John Amen.

Prolegomena to Any Future Reading of *The Folding Cliffs* / Hix

1. William Shakespeare, *The Riverside Shakespeare,* ed. G. Blakemore Evans (Boston: Houghton Mifflin, 1974), 1164

2. Michael Thurston, "The Substance of the Island: W. S. Merwin's

Lyrical Epic," *Kenyon Review* 22, nos. 3/4 (Summer/Fall 2000): 181.

3. Adam Kirsch, "The Poet's Plague," *New Republic* 220, no. 12 (March 22, 1999): 44.

4. Thurston, "Substance of the Island," 180.

5. Ibid., 181.

6. Ibid.

7. Ibid., 184.

8. Ibid.

9. Kirsch, "Poet's Plague," 44.

10. Ibid., 40.

11. Ibid., 41.

12. Ibid.

13. Ibid., 40.

14. Louis Mackey, *Faith Order Understanding: Natural Theology in the Augustinian Tradition.* (Toronto: Pontifical Institute of Mediaeval Studies, 2011), 2.

15. Ibid., 5.

16. Thurston, "Substance of the Island," 181.

17. William Wordsworth, *The Poetical Works of Wordsworth*, ed. Thomas Hutchinson (Oxford: Oxford University Press, 1933), 934.

18. Ibid., 754.

19. John Milton, *Complete Poems and Major Prose*, ed. Merritt Y. Hughes (New York: Odyssey, 1957), 212.

20. John Burt, "W. S. Merwin's *The Folding Cliffs*," *Raritan* 19, no. 3 (Winter 2000): 125.

21. Ibid., 125.

22. Ibid., 127.

23. Ibid., 125.

24. Ibid., 126.

25. Ibid., 128.

26. Ibid., 125–26.

27. Ibid., 127.

28. Ibid., 129.

29. Ibid., 133.

30. Ibid.

31. Alain Badiou, *Second Manifesto for Philosophy*, trans. Louise Burchill (Cambridge: Polity, 2011), 22.

32. Ibid., 20–21.

33. Ibid., 129.

34. Ibid., 129.

35. Ibid., 89.

Raw Shore of Paradise / Merwin, Thompson, Weinert

1. W. S. Merwin, *Present Company* (Port Townsend, WA: Copper Canyon, 2005).

2. W. S. Merwin, *The Moving Target* (New York: Atheneum, 1963).

3. W. S. Merwin, *The Rain in the Trees* (New York: Alfred A. Knopf, 1988).

4. W. S. Merwin, *The Vixen* (New York: Alfred A. Knopf, 1996).

Millennial Merwin / Kennedy

1. W. S. Merwin, *The Pupil* (New York: Alfred A. Knopf, 2001).

2. W. S. Merwin, *Present Company* (Port Townsend, WA: Copper Canyon, 2005).

3. W. S. Merwin, *The Shadow of Sirius* (Port Townsend, WA: Copper Canyon, 2008).

The Shadow of Sirius / Halliday and Theune

1. Ed Folsom and Cary Nelson, introduction to *W. S. Merwin: Essays on the Poetry*, Nelson and Folsom, eds. (Urbana: University of Illinois Press, 1987), 15.

2. Ibid.

3. W. S. Merwin, *The Shadow of Sirius* (Port Townsend, WA: Copper Canyon, 2008).

4. Folsom and Nelson, introduction, 17.

5. Edward W. Said, *On Late Style* (London: Bloomsbury, 2006), 7.

6. Ibid, 6.

7. Quoted in Frank MacShane, "A Portrait of W. S. Merwin," *Shenandoah* 21, no. 2 (Winter 1970): 7.

8. Quoted in "Appendix 2: Merwin Manuscripts in Other Collections," in *W. S. Merwin*, ed. Nelson and Folsom, 358.

9. Robert Scholes, "Reading Merwin Semiotically," in *W. S. Merwin*, ed. Nelson and Folsom, 65.

10. H. L. Hix, *Understanding W. S. Merwin* (Columbia: University of South Carolina Press, 1997), 33.

11. W. S. Merwin, *The First Four Books of Poems* (Port Townsend, WA: Copper Canyon, 2000), 139.

12. Merwin, *Travels* (New York: Alfred A. Knopf, 1994), 4.

13. Thomas B. Byers, "The Present Voices: W. S. Merwin since 1970," in Nelson and Folsom, *W. S. Merwin*, 251.

14. A partial list of these poems includes "Song," in *First Four*, 62–63; "On the Subject of Poetry," in *First Four*, 109; "Canso," in *First Four*, 131–35; "River Sound Remembered," in *First Four*, 190; "Fog," in *First Four*, 212–13; "The Frozen Sea," in *First Four*, 227; "Sailor Ashore," in *First Four*, 228; "Blind Girl," in *First Four*, 257–58; "Cuckoo Myth," in *The Second Four Books of Poems* (Port Townsend, WA: Copper Canyon, 1993), 200–201; "A Door," in *Second Four*, 245–47; "Fox Sleep," in *The Vixen* (New York: Alfred A. Knopf, 1996), 3–6; "Gate," in *Vixen*, 7; "End of a Day," in *Vixen*, 25; "The Shortest Night," in *Vixen*, 57; "The Marfa Lights," in *The Pupil* (New York: Alfred A. Knopf, 2001), 11–13; "Migrants by Night," in *Pupil*, 14–15; "To the Morning (1)," in *Present Company* (Port Townsend, WA: Copper Canyon, 2005), 71; "To a Friend Turning Fifty," in *Present Company*, 118–19; "To Paula," in *Present Company*, 131; and "Near Field," in *Shadow*, 83.

15. Other poems that feature a self-referential structural turn include "Proteus," in *First Four*, 110–12; "Fog," in *First Four*, 212–13; "Sailor Ashore," in *First Four*, 228; "The Different Stars," in *Second Four*, 136–37; "Ascent," in *Second Four*, 188; "To the Hand," in *Second Four*, 267–68; "The Flight," in *Flower and Hand: Poems 1977–1983* (Port Townsend, WA: Copper Canyon, 1996), 66; "To the Dust of the Road," in *Present Company*, 48; "To the Margin," in *Present Company*, 75, and "To the Morning (2)," in *Present Company*, 121.

16. Helen Vendler, "Defender of the Earth," *New York Review of Books* 105, no. 5 (26 March 2009): 37.

17. Ibid., 38.

18. Ibid.

19. Marjorie Perloff, "Apocalypse Then: Merwin and the Sorrows of

Literary History," in Nelson and Folsom, *W. S. Merwin*, 143.

20. Ibid., 134.

21. Ibid.

22. Ibid., 135.

23. Ibid., 136.

24. Merwin selected and introduced the poems of *The Essential Wyatt* (New York: Ecco, 1989).

25. W. S. Merwin, *Asian Figures* (New York: Atheneum, 1973), n. pag.

26. Merwin's *The Miner's Pale Children* (1970) and *Houses and Travellers* (1977) were first published by Atheneum; eventually they were published together as W. S. Merwin, *The Book of Fables* (Port Townsend, WA: Copper Canyon, 2007), 98.

27. Most notably "To My Teeth," 13, and "To a Mosquito," 91–92.

28. That Donne is the subject of Merwin's first poem is a fact noted in Mark Christhilf, "W. S. Merwin: The Poet as Creative Conservator," *Modern Age*, Spring 1979, 168.

29. Perloff, "Apocalypse Then," 129.

30. Paul Celan, "Backlight," in *Collected Prose,* trans. Rosmarie Waldrop (Riverdale-on-Hudson, NY: Sheep Meadow, 1986), 14.

31. Merwin I, 17-1444-50, Box 17, folder marked "October 1946–June, 1948," W. S. Merwin Archives, Rare Book and Manuscript Library, University of Illinois at Urbana-Champaign.

32. Su Tung-p'o, "Hsin-ch'ou Eleventh Month, Nineteenth Day," in *Selected Poems of Su Tung-p'o,* trans. Burton Watson (Port Townsend, WA: Copper Canyon, 1993), 20.

33. Barbara Herrnstein Smith, *Poetic Closure: A Study of How Poems End* (Chicago: University of Chicago Press, 1968), 206.

34. Robert von Hallberg, *Lyric Powers* (Chicago: University of Chicago Press, 2008), 2.

35. Thomas Hardy, "The Shadow on the Stone," in *The Collected Poems of Thomas Hardy* (London: Wordsworth Editions, 1998), 489.

36. Folsom and Nelson, introduction, 17.

All of Memory Waking / Harp

1. George Steiner, *Real Presences* (Chicago: University of Chicago Press, 1989), 82.

2. Walter J. Ong, *An Ong Reader: Challenges for Further Inquiry*, ed. Thomas J. Farrell and Paul A. Soukup (Cresskill, NJ: Hampton, 2002), 375.

3. Robert K. Logan, *The Extended Mind: The Emergence of Language, the Human Mind, and Culture* (Toronto: University of Toronto Press, 2007), 5 and passim.

4. Ibid., 45.

5. W. S. Merwin, *The Shadow of Sirius* (Port Townsend, WA: Copper Canyon, 2009).

6. Jay B. Holberg, *Sirius: Brightest Diamond in the Night Sky* (Chichester, UK: Praxis, 2007), 4–22.

7. Ibid., 47–98.

8. Ibid., 214–15.

9. *Eighteen Songs of a Nomad Flute: The Story of Lady Wen-Chi, a Fourteenth-Century Handscroll in the Metropolitan Museum of Art*, ed. and trans. Robert A. Rorex and Wen Fong (New York: Metropolitan Museum of Art, 1974).

10. Christian Tyler, *Wild West China: The Taming of Xinjiang* (New Brunswick, NJ: Rutgers University Press, 2004), 28–30.

11. *Oxford English Dictionary*, s.v. "measure."

12. Ibid., s.v. "versus."

13. Walter J. Ong, *Orality and Literacy: The Technologizing of the Word* (New York: Routledge, 1988), 31.

The Form of Absence / Caplan

1. T. V. F. Brogan, Lawrence J. Zillman, and Clive Scott, "Sonnet," in *The New Princeton Encyclopedia of Poetry and Poetics*, ed. Alex Preminger and T. V. F. Brogan (Princeton, NJ: Princeton University Press, 1993), 1167.

2. I borrow this phrase from Stephen Burt and David Mikics, *The Art of the Sonnet* (Cambridge, MA: Harvard University Press, 2010), 3.

3. T. S. Eliot, *Selected Prose of T S. Eliot*, ed. Frank Kermode. (New York: Farrar, Straus and Giroux, 1975), 32.

4. See, for instance, James Boswell, *Life of Johnson* (Oxford: Oxford University Press, 1980), 1079.

5. "For a Coming Extinction: Joel Whitney interviews W. S. Merwin," *Guernica*, February 2011, available at http://www.guernicamag.com/in-

terviews/2367/merwin_2_15_11/I. I wish to thank Jeanie Thompson for bringing the interview to my attention.

6. W. S. Merwin, *The Shadow of Sirius* (Port Townsend, WA: Copper Canyon, 2009), 26–27.

7. Robert Frost, *The Collected Prose of Robert Frost*, ed. Mark Richardson (Cambridge, MA: Harvard University Press, 2007), 116.

8. Merwin, "For a Coming Extinction."

9. H. L. Hix, *Understanding W. S. Merwin* (Columbia: University of South Carolina Press, 1997), vii.

10. Ibid. 90–91.

11. Ibid. 91, 92.

12. H. L. Hix, *Chromatic* (Youngstown, OH: Etruscan, 2006), 48.

13. Debra Allbery, *Fimbul-Winter* (New York: Four Way Books, 2010), 38.

14. Eve Grubin, *Morning Prayer* (Riverdale-on-Hudson, NY: Sheep Meadow, 2005), 45.

15. Eve Grubin, e-mail correspondence, October 30, 2011.

Acknowledgments

"On the Subject of Poetry," "The Animals," "When You Go Away," and "Exercise" from *Migration* by W. S. Merwin. Copyright © 1954, 1967, 1973, 2005 by W. S. Merwin, used by permission of The Wylie Agency LLC. "Plane" from *The Second Four Books of Poems* by W. S. Merwin. Copyright © 1993 by W. S. Merwin, used by permission of The Wylie Agency LLC. Excerpts from "Finding a Teacher," "Gift," and "The Last One" from *Migration* by W. S. Merwin. Copyright © 1967, 1973, 2005 by W. S. Merwin, used by permission of The Wylie Agency LLC.

"Most of the Stories have to Do with Vanishing" by Matthew Zapruder first appeared in *American Poet,* the journal of the Academy of American Poets.

"Raw Shore of Paradise: A Conversation with W. S. Merwin," by Jeanie Thompson and Jonathan Weinert, originally appeared in *The Louisville Review,* Number 61, Fall 2007. www.louisvillereview.org

"The Act Finds the Utterance: W. S. Merwin's 'Substance'," by Forrest Gander, first appeared in *Many Mountains Moving,* Volume 14, No. 2, July 2001.

W. S. Merwin, "Just This," "Worn Words," "Youth," "The Mole," "Nocturne," "My Hand," "One of the Butterflies," and "No" from *The Shadow of Sirius.* Copyright © 2008 by W. S. Merwin. "To the Margin," "To _____,"

About the Contributors

David Caplan is the author of *Questions of Possibility: Contemporary Poetry and Poetic Form* (Oxford University Press, 2004), *Poetic Form: An Introduction* (Pearson Longman, 2006), and *In the World He Created According to His Will* (University of Georgia Press, 2010), a book of poems. Associate professor of English and associate director of Creative Writing at Ohio Wesleyan University, Caplan is also a contributing editor to the *Virginia Quarterly Review* and *Pleiades: A Journal of New Writing*.

Steven Cramer is the author of *The Eye That Desires to Look Upward* (Galileo, 1987), *The World Book* (Copper Beech, 1992), *Dialogue for the Left and Right Hand* (Lumen Editions, 1997), *Goodbye to the Orchard* (Sarabande Books, 2004)—a Massachusetts Honor Book and winner of the Sheila Motton Prize from the New England Poetry Club—and *Clangings* (Sarabande Books, 2012). His work is represented in *The Autumn House Anthology of Contemporary America Poetry, Villanelles* (Everyman's Library Pocket Poets Series), and other anthologies. Recipient of Massachusetts Arts Council and NEA fellowships, Cramer directs the MFA program at Lesley University.

Debra Kang Dean is the author of *News of Home* (1998) and *Precipitates* (2003), both from BOA Editions. "In the Valley of Its Saying," a personal essay, is included in *The Colors of Nature: Culture, Identity, and the Natural World* (Milkweed Editions, 2011). Dean teaches in the brief-residency

MFA in Writing Program at Spalding University and currently lives in Bloomington, Indiana.

Forrest Gander was born in the Mojave Desert and grew up, for the most part, in Virginia. He has degrees in geology and English literature. His recent books include the novel *As a Friend* (2008) and the book of poems *Core Samples from the World* (2011), both from New Directions. His most recent translations include Pura López Colomé's Villaurrutia Award–winning book *Watchword* (Wesleyan University Press, 2012) and, with Kyoko Yoshida, *Spectacle & Pigsty: Selected Poems of Kiwao Nomura* (Omnidawn, 2011). A United States Artists Rockefeller Fellow, Gander is recipient of fellowships from the NEA and the Guggenheim, Howard, and Whiting Foundations.

Mark Halliday teaches at Ohio University. His books of poems are *Little Star* (William Morrow, 1987), *Tasker Street* (University of Massachusetts Press, 1992), *Selfwolf* (University of Chicago Press, 1999), *Jab* (University of Chicago Press, 2002), and *Keep This Forever* (Tupelo Press, 2008). His study of Wallace Stevens, *Stevens and the Interpersonal*, was published in 1991 by Princeton University Press. He has published many essays on contemporary poets including Claire Bateman, Joshua Clover, Carl Dennis, Tony Hoagland, David Kirby, August Kleinzahler, Kenneth Koch, Larry Levis, Mary Ruefle, and James Tate.

Jerry Harp's books of poems are *Creature* (Salt, 2003), *Gatherings* (Ashland Poetry, 2004), and *Urban Flowers, Concrete Plains* (Salt, 2006). His *For Us, What Music? The Life and Poetry of Donald Justice* (University of Iowa Press) and *Constant Motion: Ongian Hermeneutics and the Shifting Ground of Early Modern Understanding* (Hampton Press) both appeared in 2010. Harp teaches at Lewis & Clark College.

H. L. Hix's most recent books are a "selected poems," *First Fire, Then Birds: Obsessionals 1985–2010* (Etruscan, 2010); a translation, made with the author, of Eugenijus Ališanka's *from unwritten histories* (Host, 2011); and an essay collection, *Lines of Inquiry* (Etruscan, 2011). His website is www.hlhix.com.

Mark Irwin is the author of six collections of poetry, most recently *White City* (BOA Editions, 2000), *Bright Hunger* (BOA Editions, 2004), and *Tall If* (New Issues, 2008). His *American Urn: New & Selected Poems (1987–2011)* will appear in 2012 from Ashland University Poetry Press. He lives in Colorado and Los Angeles, where he teaches in the PhD in Literature and Creative Writing Program at the University of Southern California.

Sarah Kennedy is the author of six books of poems, including *Home Remedies* (LSU Press, 2009), *A Witch's Dictionary* (Elixir, 2008), *Consider the Lilies* (David Robert Books, 2004), *Double Exposure* (Cleveland State University Poetry Center, 2003), and *Flow Blue* (Elixir, 2002). Her seventh, *The Gold Thread*, is due out from Elixir Press in 2012. A professor at Mary Baldwin College in Staunton, Virginia, Kennedy has received grants from the NEA and the Virginia Commission for the Arts. She is currently a contributing editor for *West Branch* and *Shenandoah*.

Eric Pankey is the author of eight collections of poetry, most recently *The Pear as One Example: New and Selected Poems, 1984–2008* (Ausable / Copper Canyon, 2008). Two new collections are forthcoming from Milkweed Editions. He teaches in the Master of Fine Arts Program at George Mason University.

Lisa Russ Spaar is the author of several books of poems, most recently *Vanitas, Rough*, forthcoming from Persea Books in 2012. Her awards include a Rona Jaffe Award for Emerging Women Writers and a Guggenheim Fellowship. She is editor of *Acquainted with the Night: Insomnia Poems* (Columbia University Press, 1999) and *All That Mighty Heart: London Poems* (University of Virginia Press, 2008). Spaar is poetry editor of the *Chronicle of Higher Education Review* and teaches at the University of Virginia.

Michael Theune is the editor of *Structure and Surprise: Engaging Poetic Turns* (Teachers & Writers, 2007) and the host of the blog structureandsurprise.wordpress.com. Theune is a contributing editor at *Pleiades: A Journal of New Writing*, and his poems, essays, and reviews have appeared in numerous other publications, including journals such as *College English*, *Iowa Review*, and *Jacket*, and books such as *Mentor and*

Muse: From Poets to Poets (Southern Illinois University Press, 2010) and *The Monkey & the Wrench: Essays into Contemporary Poetics* (University of Akron Press, 2011). He teaches at Illinois Wesleyan University.

Jeanie Thompson has published three chapbooks and four poetry collections, including *How to Enter the River* (Holy Cow!, 1985), *Witness* (Black Belt, 1995), *White for Harvest: New and Selected Poems* (River City, 2000), and *The Seasons Bear Us* (River City, 2009). She has received artist fellowships from the Louisiana Arts Council (1982) and the Alabama State Council on the Arts (1989, 2011), and was named alumni artist of the year by the University of Alabama College of Arts and Sciences (2003). Founding director of the award-winning Alabama Writers' Forum, she also teaches in Spalding University's brief-residency MFA Writing Program.

Matthew Zapruder is the author of three collections of poetry, most recently *Come On All You Ghosts* (Copper Canyon, 2010). He has received a Guggenheim Fellowship, a William Carlos Williams Award, a May Sarton Award from the Academy of American Arts and Sciences, and a Lannan Literary Fellowship. Currently he works as an editor for Wave Books and teaches as a member of the core faculty of UCR–Palm Desert's Low Residency MFA in Creative Writing. He lives in San Francisco.

About the Photographer

Robin Holland is a portrait photographer based in New York City. Her work has been featured on the Sundance Channel and in exhibitions at George Eastman House (Rochester), P. S. 1 (a MoMA satellite in Long Island City), White Columns (New York City), the Berlin Film Festival, and the Walter Reade Gallery at Lincoln Center (as part of the 44th New York Film Festival). She has a B.A. in literature and creative writing from the State University of New York at Binghamton, where she was introduced to the work of W. S. Merwin. Many years later, she photographed Merwin for the PBS series *Bill Moyers Journal*—and then sat in the studio for the rest of the interview to hear Merwin read his work. To see more of her portraits, visit her website at www.robinholland.com.